THE GUIDE TO
MYSTERIOUS
IONA
AND STAFFA

THE GUIDE TO
MYSTERIOUS
IONA
AND STAFFA

GEOFF HOLDER

The
History
Press

In loving memory of
Sheila Holder
1930-2006

First published 2007

Reprinted in 2011 by
The History Press
The Mill, Brimscombe Port,
Stroud, Gloucestershire, GL5 2QG
www.thehistorypress.co.uk

© Geoff Holder 2011

British Library Cataloguing in Publication Data.
A catalogue record for this book is available from the British Library.

ISBN 978 0 7524 4380 5

Typesetting and origination by Tempus Publishing Limited
Printed and bound in Great Britain by
Marston Book Services Limited, Didcot

CONTENTS

Acknowledgements   6

Introduction   7

1   Saints Columba and Adomnan   15

2   Legends and Folkore   22

3   The Village   29

4   Reilig Odhráin and St Oran's Chapel   38

5   The Abbey Complex   47

6   The North of the Island   80

7   The West of the Island   94

8   The South of the Island   101

9   Staffa   113

Appendix: some notes on Iona and Staffa in popular culture   122

Bibliography   123

Index   127

ACKNOWLEDGEMENTS

I would like to thank: the Local Studies staff at the A.K. Bell Library, Perth for their diligence and help; antiquarian bookseller Lesley Fraser for the loan of a crucial book; Shona Walker and Gordon Rutherford of Historic Scotland, Iona Abbey for help and assistance above and beyond; Historic Scotland for permission to use photographs taken at their properties; Karen Turner and Richard Sharples of the Iona Community for their time and patience and for allowing me access to the Community's library; Andy Robertson for designing the maps; and Ségolène Dupuy for photography, driving and all-round encouragement. Photographs on pages 55 (lower), 56-58, 61-64, 66-68, 74, 75, 118 and 121 are by Ségolène Dupuy, as are the top right and left photos on the front cover, and centre and right images on the back cover; the rest are by the author.

For more information visit www.geoffholder.co.uk

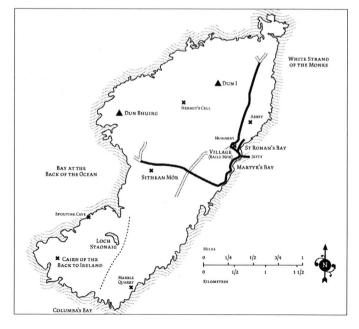

Map of Iona.

INTRODUCTION

History and legend meet here: the secular and the holy join forces, and the fabric and geography conspire.

Frank Delaney, *A Walk To The Western Isles*

I never come to Iona without the feeling that 'some god is in this place'.

Kenneth Clark, *Civilisation*

In the isle of dreams God shall yet fulfil himself anew.

Old Gaelic prophecy

A traveller was asked by an old Highland gardener where she had been. When she told him he said, 'Ay! Iona is a very thin place'. What did he mean, she asked? 'There's no' much between Iona and the Lord'. The notion of the 'thin place' – this example is from Evelyn Underhill's *Collected Papers,* but it is often repeated in other contexts – is probably one of the most persistent approaches people take to Iona. It has served individuals from a wide range of Christian, para-Christian and non-Christian beliefs, all of whom have come here looking for their particular spiritual experience. Iona can impact on people in striking ways. William H. Cohea Jr, a retired Presbyterian minister, wandered into the hills of the island and had a dream of being surrounded by a circle of standing stones; it was frightening, but also comforting. In the years since 1975, he has built a spiritual retreat and meditation centre called Columcille near the Upper Mount Bethel Township, Bangor, Pennsylvania. The site consists of 17 acres (9 hectares) filled with standing stones, a stone circle, Thor's Gate (a trilithon gateway), an eight-sided stone chapel to St Columba, and the St Oran Bell Tower, modelled on extant eighth-century Irish bell towers.

This book will take you through the enduring influence of Saints Columba and Adomnan, followed by a number of key supernatural and folkloric themes, and then a geographical guide to the mysterious, strange and curious aspects of the village, the Abbey, and the north, west and south of the island. At the end a separate chapter is devoted to the astonishing Isle of Staffa. Things worth seeing are asterisked, from ★ to ★★★, according to my own rating of their importance or significance.

THE SETTING

Outside the inhabited low-lying areas in the east and centre of the island, Iona's landscape is dominated by rocky outcrops, moorland and minor hills interspersed with numerous miniature glens. Be prepared for wet conditions underfoot – the bogs will suck the boots from your feet (I prefer Wellingtons). Iona can be very wet and windy - on 4 October 1860 a hurricane carried away chickens from the coops and sheaves of corn and bere from the fields and left them high and dry on the rocks of Mull without once touching the raging sea. If exploring off the minis-cule road system take a map. The best is the Colin Baxter map, widely available on the island, although I usually supplement this with the 1:25000 Ordnance Survey Explorer map 373. Six-figure OS map numbers are given where appropriate.

PLACENAMES

Adomnan's seventh-century *Life of Columba* (see Chapter 1) has influenced suc-ceeding generations to such a degree that for centuries pilgrims, visitors and islanders have, consciously or otherwise, been on a mission to match what they see with what has been written. As a consequence the geography of Iona has been mythologised and Columban placenames imprinted on the landscape. A few placenames have good documentary or archaeological support; some are almost certainly relatively modern associations; and others are lost in the abyss of what is ubiquitously called 'tradition'. It may therefore be useful to think of Columban names – and their associated stories – as being in a spectrum of credibility. So Tòrr an Aba and St Columba's Shrine have a high level of credibility, while Columba's Table and Columba's Stone are at the fantasy end of the spectrum. The Hermit's Cell and Port of the Coracle probably occupy a halfway point on the scale. Of course, whether or not a Columban association is *actually* true or not is irrelevant to the fact that people *believe* it is true, and behave in a certain way because of that belief: expectations shape behaviour. So, pilgrims built cairns of stones at Columba's Bay because they believed that is where he landed; and modern visitors meditate at the Hermit's Cell because of a persistent belief that Columba did the same.

CHRONOLOGY

c. 565:   Columba arrives on Iona and founds monastery.
574:         Columba consecrates Aidan as King of Dalriada, first instance of a Scottish monarch being legitimised by a Christian ceremony.

597:        Columba dies.

c. 697:   Adomnan writes his *Life of Columba*.

Eighth/ninth centuries: High Crosses erected.

795:        First Danish Viking attack.

802:        Vikings burn wooden monastery.

806:        Vikings kill sixty-eight monks.

807:        Columba's grave opened and his bones removed; start of extensive travels of different sets of relics – bones, books, accoutrements – between Iona, various parts of Ireland, and mainland Scotland.

814:        Abbot Cellach transfers the primacy of the monastery to a new foundation in Kells. Iona continues to be inhabited despite repeated Viking attacks.

Early ninth century: monastery rebuilt in stone.

825:        Viking massacre of monks; St Blathmac martyred.

From mid-ninth century: Norwegian Vikings effectively rule the Isles.

845:        Viking raid.

849/851:   Some of Columba's relics help establish Kenneth MacAlpin's power base in Dunkeld, Perthshire.

878:        Viking raid.

Tenth/twelfth century: Old Irish *Life of Columba* and *Life of Adomnan* written.

904:        Constantin, King of Alban, defeats a Viking force in Strathearn, Perthshire with Columba's crozier as his standard and guarantee of battle magic.

980:        Olaf Cuaran, Scandinavian king of Dublin, on pilgrimage to Iona, dies and is buried on the island; possibly not the first king interred on Iona.

986:        Viking massacre of the Abbot and fifteen monks.

1098:   King Magnus Barelegs of Norway plunders the Isles but spares Iona.

1156:   Establishment of the Lordship of the Isles, sea-kings in all but name. Until 1266, when Norway cedes the Western Isles and gives up claims to this part of Scotland, the Lords play off the Scottish and Norwegian kings against each other.

Mid-twelfth century: St Oran's chapel built. Start of the tradition of the Lords of the Isles and the noble families of the West Coast being buried in Reilig Odhráin.

1164:   Community of Culdee hermits recorded at Iona, probably living alongside but separate from the main monastery.

c.1200-1204: Establishment of Benedictine Abbey and Augustinian Nunnery by Reginald, Lord of the Isles. Latin Christendom displaces Irish Christianity. Attempted coup by Irish churchmen fails. End of an era.

1210:   Norwegian pirates plunder Iona.

Fourteenth century onwards: Lords of the Isles increasingly involved in the politics of mainland Scotland.

1314:   Relic of St Columba assures Robert the Bruce's victory over Edward II of England at the Battle of Bannockburn.

Fifteenth century: Maclean's Cross erected.

1493:   Lordship of the Isles forfeited to the Scottish crown. Periodic rebellions last until 1545.

1499:   Iona established as the Cathedral of the Isles, base of the Bishop of the Isles.

1532:   Manus O'Donnell writes the fantasy-rich *Life of Colum-cille*.

1549:   First contemporary description of Iona, by Donald Munro, Dean of the Isles.

1560:   Reformation. Peaceful in Iona. Some monks continue to live in the Abbey for two decades.

Sixteenth century: Abbey owned by the Maclean Clan of Duart.

Seventeenth century: the Campbell Dukes of Argyll acquire Iona. Abbey in ruins.

1772:   Sir Joseph Banks 'discovers' Staffa.

Nineteenth century: Iona and Staffa become major tourist attractions.

1875:   Some consolidation and repairs to the Abbey.

1899:   The eighth Duke of Argyll transfers Iona's historic monuments to the Iona Cathedral Trust, with the proviso that they must be open to Christians of all persuasions.

Early twentieth century: some rebuilding of the Abbey.

1938:   Revd George MacLeod founds the Iona Community as an ecumenical Christian community. Over next few decades rebuilding and restoration continues under both the Iona Community and the Iona Cathedral Trust.

2000:   Iona Cathedral Trust transfers ownership of all the ecclesiastical monuments to Historic Scotland.

KEY CONCEPTS:

Apotropaic –   Protective against evil.

Fairies –   Placenames featuring the Gaelic word 'sith' (pronounced 'shee') are generally taken to mark an association with the fairies. 'Sithean' and 'Sidhean' ('shee-an') usually indicate fairy knolls or hills.

Liminality –   That which is betwixt and between, a transition, a threshold. Very important in magic and encountering the supernatural. Liminality can apply to places (caves, bogs, rivers, boundaries) or times - Hallowe'en, Hogmanay, Beltane (1 May).

Magical Thinking – 1. Certain things (a saint's relics, water from a special source, an unusual stone) have power. 2. This power can be accessed through proximity to the source. (So rich people paid large sums to be buried in church, the closer to the altar (the power source) the better.) 3. Things which have been connected once are connected for ever ('sympathetic magic').

Simulacra –   Natural formations in trees and rocks which we, pattern-seeking apes that we are, interpret as faces, animals and 'Signs from God'.

Storytelling –   Our species is misnamed – *Homo sapiens* (wise human) should be *Pan narrans,* the storytelling ape. It is in our nature to take a chaotic series of events and turn it into a *story.* We do it all the time in our daily lives. Paranormal events are often random and confusing, but they quickly become transformed into a *ghost story.* Moral: don't depend on stories if you're looking for truth.

'Tradition' –   Also known as 'it is said that', 'they say that', and other get-outs used by writers to bring a spurious gravitas to tall tales. Treat with caution.

'Truth' –   Just because a respected chronicler from a previous age has written something down, doesn't make it true. And I'm often reporting the words of storytellers, fantasists, liars and journalists. *Caveat lector.*

A NOTE ON SOURCES

Iona's isolation from the mainstream of Scottish life from medieval times onward means that from the sixteenth to the early nineteenth centuries we are dependent on the writings of a relatively small number of travellers. As these are referred to again and again they are simply mentioned in the text as Martin, Pococke, Pennant etc. They are:

Munro: Sir Donald Munro, High Dean of the Isles, visited Iona 1549, wrote
               A Description of the Western Isles of Scotland (published 1774).
Sacheverell: William Sacheverell, Governor of the Isle of Man, wrote *An Account
               of the Isle of Man, with a Voyage to I-columb-kill in the year 1688* (1702).
Martin: Martin Martin, a Skye doctor who toured the Hebrides in 1695,
               publishing *A Description of the Western Isles of Scotland* (1703).
Pococke: Richard Pococke, Bishop of Ossory, Ireland, visited Iona in June
               1760, but his manuscripts were not published (as *Pococke's Tours in
               Scotland*) until 1887.
Pennant: Thomas Pennant, Fellow of the Royal Society, published *A Tour of
               Scotland and a Voyage to the Hebrides (1772)*.
Walker: Revd Dr John Walker, commissioned by the Commission for
               Annexed Estates and the Church of Scotland to report on the state
               of education, religion and the economy in the Hebrides, wrote
               Report on the Hebrides of 1764 and 1771.

OTHER SOURCES

By the nineteenth century regular steamships brought tourists to the islands, and
there are many travellers' accounts from this time on. Boat schedules and weather
meant most visitors spent just a few hours on Iona; their information came from
local self-appointed guides, who sometimes mixed fact, speculation and legend
without discrimination – many of the current beliefs associated with Iona probably derive from this source.

Every writer on Iona owes a debt to historian William Skene's three-volume
Celtic Scotland of 1876-1880; although many of its arguments have been super-
seded it was hugely influential in its day.

Many Victorian ecclesiastics wrote learnedly about Iona, but sometimes their
overt ideological position (for example, pro-Culdees or anti-Catholic) means
their works have to be used with caution.

There are many references in this book to the works of Fiona Macleod, for
whom Iona was a lodestone. In her writings she mentioned having been born on
Iona, which puzzled the islanders as no one could remember Ms Macleod. There
was good reason for this, as 'Fiona' was William Sharp, a literary critic from Paisley,
who spoke very little Gaelic and visited the island in 1894 when most of the population were native Gaelic-speakers. His secret was kept until his death in 1905
– he even wrote a fake biography for Fiona in *Who's Who*. Sharp did not arbitrar-
ily choose this female pseudonym; Fiona was a definitely female inner voice who
took him over and allowed him to write mystical prose that he could never nor-
mally attempt; Sharp seemed to regard her at times as a separate, discarnate entity.
Her style is very much a matter of taste – either you think it is poetic, allusive
and moving, or you regard it as the very worst kind of Celtic Twilight claptrap.

Macleod/Sharp deserves credit for recording and making sense of a great many folktales and beliefs, but it is often difficult to tell whether a particular episode is folkloric, factual, or a fiction.

Alec and Euphemia Ritchie's *Iona Past and Present* (first published in 1928) has a superb map with many placenames (compiled by David Munro Fraser) which are not found on any of the commonly available modern maps.

Otta Swire's *The Inner Hebrides and Their Legends* (1964) contains a wealth of folkloric material not found elsewhere, although it is not referenced and certainly some of it is fanciful.

Donald MacCulloch's *Staffa* (1975, first edition 1927) provided much of the information for the chapter on that island.

The vast majority of the archaeological, architectural and sculptural information has come from the monumental *Argyll: An Inventory of the Monuments, Volume 4: Iona* (referred to in the text as *Argyll 4*) by the Royal Commission on Ancient and Historical Monuments in Scotland, backed up by Canmore, the RCAHMS online site (www.rcahms.gov.uk), as well as Steer and Bannerman's *Late Medieval Sculpture in the West Highlands*, and Anna Ritchie's *Iona*.

I would also like to pay tribute to a wonderful writer, E. Mairi MacArthur, whose books are quoted extensively in these pages.

These and all other works mentioned can be found in the bibliography.

NOTE

Iona has been known by several names, notably Hy, I, Y, I-colm-kill, I-columb-cille and other similar variants (Columcille being the Gaelic version of Columba). Unless quoting someone, I have just used the modern name.

1

SAINTS COLUMBA
AND ADOMNAN

ST COLUMBA

With the best will in the world, we cannot rediscover the full historical reality of any saint. Hindsight has been too thoroughly spiritualised, and has become the main driving force of saintly business.

Donald E. Meek, *Between faith and folklore*

Columba dominates the early history of Iona. An Irish prince who had chosen the route of the church when Christianity in Ireland was still competing against paganism, he was already in his forties – old by Dark Ages standards – with a lifetime of founding monasteries and astute political-religious diplomacy behind him when he arrived on Iona around the year 575. This was a beachhead mission to support the nascent Christian Irish kingdom of Dalriada in west Scotland. Militarily beleaguered by Pictish and other pagan neighbours, Dalriada was in crisis and Columba's combination of warrior-monk intellectual ferocity and personal charisma was just what the Dalriadans ordered. When, in his seventies, he died in 597, Iona was a beacon of Christian civilisation and learning whose political and sacred power continued to influence Scottish life for centuries. However, there are many books and guides which will give you details of Columba's life and achievements so I do not intend to repeat that information here. Rather, we will look at the way Columba the man became Columba the stuff of legend, folklore and magic.

There were a great many adventurous, clever, brave and successful pagan-converting holy men operating in Scotland in the sixth and seventh centuries. Columba is the most famous because, arguably, he had the best PR campaign. A century after Columba's death Adomnan, ninth Abbot of Iona, wrote his *Life of Columba*. Where most saints' *Lives* have either been lost or have faded into scholarly obscurity, Adomnan's *Life of Columba* is still in print and widely read. It is our primary source for information on Columba and monastic Iona. There are other, even earlier sources, and a cauldron-full of later works, and because so many stories circulate around Columba it is important to

Statue of St Columba on the
Bishop's House.

know the source, and how far back it goes. So here is a chronological guide to
the way how, from the very start, the written word mythologised Columba and
developed his cult.

597.   Columba dies.

600.   The *Amra choluimb chille*, 'The Elegy of Colum cille' composed. The
        author, the monk Dallan, writes about miracles and weather magic at
        Columba's grave. Columba is described as speaking with angels and
        apostles, and his sonorous voice could be heard 1500 paces away. Already
        within three years of his death Columba has a supernormal reputation.

623-52. Abbot Segene gathers the testimony of monks and lay people regard-
        ing Columba's power and holiness. The Christian King Oswald of
        Northumbria told Segene of his vision of a gigantic Columba 'radiant
        in angelic form, whose lofty height seemed with its head to touch the
        clouds…and standing in the midst of the camp he covered it with his
        shining raiment'. The next day, under the protection of the saint, Oswald
        defeated Cadwallon near Hexham. The year was 633. The monk Failbe
        (later Abbot of Iona) was present when Oswald told Segene this, and
        Failbe in turn repeated the description to his successor Adomnan. This
        is the first example of Columba's posthumous role in providing battle
        magic.

c. 650.   Beccán mac Luigdech writes two poems praising Columba, who will protect Beccán from danger during life and from hell after death.

657-669.   Segene's nephew and successor as Abbot, Cummene, compiles an account of Columba's virtues and miracles.

c. 690s.   Adomnan (Abbot 679-704) writes *Life of Columba,* incorporating Cummene's work. First-time readers of this astonishing irruption from the Dark Ages Christian mind are often surprised to find it is explicitly supernatural in both tone and content. As John Smith (*The Life of Columba*) wrote in 1798, 'Unhappily, it seems not to have been the object of those good men to delineate the real life and character of the saint, but to give a marvelous detail of visions, prophecies, and miracles, which they boldly ascribe to him. It is but candid to suppose that they themselves believed what they wrote, and that their writings may have been of use in those ages of credulity and fable; although, in our more enlightened times, they rather disgust than edify in that antiquated form'. There have been several translations of the *Life*; the most accessible are by Marsden and Sharpe (both 1995).

In Adomnan's *Life,* Columba:

Prophesised the achievements of various saints.

Was aware of events in far-off places and sometimes influenced those events.

Had precognition of minor local incidents in the very near future.

Had foreknowledge of others' deaths, or accurately predicted their long life, prosperity and fame.

Achieved miracles in Ireland by remote control from Iona.

Communicated at a distance.

Was privy to 'the secret things that have been hidden since the world began'.

Foresaw his own death.

Controlled the weather.

Protected his people against plague.

Cursed people and animals to death and caused ships to sink.

Raised people from the dead.

Healed people – often with just the hem of his robe or by using something blessed by him.

Made a tree produce sweet apples.

Changed water into wine.

Conversed with angels.

Bested Druids and sorcerers in magical contests.

Enabled fishermen to catch huge fish.

Shrivelled the hand of a monk who had sheltered and ordained his lover, a known murderer.

Gave a poor man a stake that miraculously caused food animals to impale themselves on it.

Exorcized a demon in a milk pail.

Subdued a monster in the River Ness.

Arrived in Iona with twelve disciples.

Miraculously increased herds of cattle.

Deflected an assassin's spear with his woollen white cowl.

Was whipped by an angel until he agreed to crown Aidan king of Dalriada.

Prayed successfully for Aidan's victory in battle.

Fought with demons seeking to take souls.

Blessed a knife that would harm neither man nor beast. The monks melted it down and coated all the tools in the monastery so they could not be used for harm.

Opened locked gates and buildings with the sign of the cross.

Had a voice which struck terror and amazement in his enemies at a great distance.

Was frequently illuminated by heavenly light.

Saved a marriage by praying for the wife to love and sleep with her husband.

Safely rode in a chariot whose lynch-pins were lethally unsecured.

Struck water out of a rock.

Purified a poisoned/bedevilled well.

Transported objects through time and space.

Saw angels carrying holy men to heaven, often battling against demons.

Fought against vicious demons.

In addition, Adomnan mentions various signs and wonders prophesying Columba's birth, and his posthumous powers. Even sinful men who recited poetry in praise of Columba escaped their enemies 'through flames and swords and spears'. Angels were frequently seen at his grave. Books written by him had miraculous powers – they were laid on the altar when prayers were said for favourable winds, they ended droughts, and were resistant to immersion in water. When he died the eastern part of the night sky in Donegal lit up with a pillar of fire.

So, in the oldest and most authoritative book we have on Columba, we find telepathy, remote viewing, teleportation, telekinesis, precognition, exorcism, fairy-tale wizardry, death curses, illumination, sympathetic magic, angelology, demonology, weather, love and battle magic, remote healing, New Testament miracles, apotropaic rituals and mastery of life and death. John Smith wrote: 'of those marvelous relations I do not profess to believe any; nor would I be so bold as to deny them all'.

Next in terms of antiquity is the *Betha Coluim Cille*, the *Life of Columba* in Old Irish. The original text is tenth or eleventh century, although the earliest extant copy is in the *Leabar Breac* of 1397 (it is reprinted in Skene's *Celtic Scotland* of 1877). Unlike Adomnan's *Life*, this purports to be a chronological, cradle-to-grave biography. It is very Irish-centric, relocating many of Adomnan's Scottish stories to Ireland, and adding a great deal of specifically Irish material. It also creates a whole new raft of magic, omens, miracles and prophecies which demonstrate how Columba's legend and cult had grown in the centuries after his death.

By 1263 the saint had become established within Scandinavian tradition. In *Hakon's Saga*, Alexander II of Scotland, on his way to attack King Hakon's fleet in 1249 after committing atrocities against the Gaelic-Norse Hebridean peoples under Columba's protection, had a vision of a towering, wrathful Columba accompanied by St Olaf of Norway and St Magnus of Orkney. Here, Columba has taken on some of the malign aspects of the Norse war god Odin.

In the fourteenth century the monks on Inchcolm Island in the Firth of Forth were chanting the Inchcolm Antiphoner:

> Mouth of the dumb,
> Light of the blind,
> Foot of the lame,
> To the fallen stretch out your hand.
> Strengthen the senseless,
> Restore the mad.
> O Columba, hope of Scots,
> By your merits' mediation,
> Make us companions
> Of the blessed angels.

Then in 1532 another *Betha Colaim Chille* (*Life of Columba*) was compiled by Manus O'Donnell, a major figure in northwest Renaissance Ireland. It is a compendium of legends and apocrypha and seems to be the legacy of several centuries of Columba's perceived power seeping into folklore and everyday apotropaic rituals, as recorded almost a thousand years after the death of the saint. A recent editor, Brian Lacey, describes it as a sort of cross between 'an historical novel and a collection of folk traditions'. It is the Old Irish and O'Donnell *Lives* that provide the basis for most of the popular stories about Columba, and in terms of accuracy neither can be trusted. For example, if you have read elsewhere that Columba was forced into exile from Ireland for his part in the slaughter at the battle of Culdrevny following a copyright infringement dispute, then look to O'Donnell for the origin – it is not mentioned in earlier works. Similarly, many of the things people 'know' about Columba can be traced to O'Donnell's compilation.

In *Carmina Gadelica* (1900), the treasury of Hebridean folklore and incantations collected by Alexander Carmichael, the saint is a protector of the weak and an all-purpose insurance for the tasks of everyday life. He is invoked for milking, churning, herding, reaping, calving, hunting and weaving, and against disease, toothache and the evil eye. His plant (St John's wort), when secretly kept in the armpit or hidden in clothes, wards off 'second sight, enchantment, witchcraft, evil eye and death' and brings peace, prosperity and fertility. He heals (and speaks to) a wounded swan from Ireland and helps a poor widow. He is 'just and potent', 'beneficent, benign', 'apostle of shore and sea', although also 'Columcille of the graves and tombs' and the way he is frequently addressed as 'gentle' suggests a parallel with the amelioratory language used for the fairies ('the Good People') and hints that Columba had a darker side that needed to be placated. He curses all the cocks in a town that had offended him, so that they never crow again. Cattle being driven are requested 'the protection of Odhran the dun...and the sanctuary of Colum Cille.' Columba is invoked along with the Virgin, Michael, other angels, the apostles, St Patrick, St Bride and 'Adomnan of laws'. He converses with Christ and John the Baptist. Columba was said to have been born on 7 December 521, and Thursday was a day of good omen to start any activity, to cure the mad – or to give birth or die.

On Iona, Sacheverell and Martin both record the bizarre story of the 'Clan vic n' oster' (from the Latin, *ostiarii,* door-keepers). The family had held the office of porter in Columba's day. Somehow they displeased him and were cursed to never exceed eight (or five) in number. Martin said whenever anyone in the family gave birth the other four were afraid of death. And perhaps inevitably, a death did occur quickly. The man Martin met was supposedly the very last of his line.

ST ADOMNAN

Adomnan himself was no slouch when it came to legends and folklore, many of them centring around the proclamation in 697 of the Cáin Adomnáin, 'Adomnan's Law'. This deeply humanitarian work protected women and other non-combatants from the brutality of Dark Ages warfare in Ireland. Adomnan not only laid it down as the law, he got dozens of warlords and chiefs to sign up to it, an indication of his status and diplomatic skills. Later notes and glosses add the supernatural inspiration and authority for the Cáin Adomnáin. In one, the Virgin Mary herself urges Adomnan to promote the Law. In another, Adomnan raises from the dead a woman slain in battle and learns her woes. As a result he goes on hunger strike and is buried alive (by his mother) for four years. Angels arrive with instructions from God to come to the surface but Adomnan faces the Almighty down until 'women are freed for me'. When some recalcitrant kings challenge the Law they are cursed with the 'Bell of Adomnan's Wrath' – not only do they die but their bloodline does also. In the tenth century *Fis Adamnain,* or *Vision of Adomnan,* the saint, described as 'the High Scholar of the Western World', is, on the feast of John the Baptist, taken in spirit by St Michael the Archangel on a voyage through heaven, purgatory and hell. This precursor of Dante's *Divine Comedy* was supposedly a vision Adomnan experienced on the eve of the great synod of Birr where he proclaimed the Cáin Adomnáin. The portrait of Adomnan as a supernaturally powerful and frightening figure in these works (his name can be translated as 'man of great dread') is continued in the tenth century *Life of Adomnan*. He brings the Pictish king Bruide mac Bili back from the dead, but reverses the process when another monk suggests this miracle sets too high a standard for future Abbots. He has the power to control events through prophecy. His relics are brought out to exorcize a demon. In a medieval manuscript held in Brussels, obviously written retrospectively, Columba prophesies the coming of a saint who will be his own kinsman, who will make a law for women. And in Glen Lyon, Perthshire, Adomnan averted a plague by causing the disease to burrow itself into a rock. By 697 Adomnan was in his seventies and retired to Ireland. Having received a premonition of his death (just as Columba had) he returned to Iona in 704 aged seventy-seven. In 727 his relics were taken on a circuit of Irish churches to settle tribal disputes and renew the Law.

BUILD-YOURSELF-A-SAINT KIT

In his essay 'Between faith and folklore', Donald E. Meek writes that, 'since at least the first centenary of his death, Columba has been the flexible friend of a wide variety of seekers and, of course, finders who have not hesitated to use his good offices for their own earthly purposes'. The Columba you want is the Columba you get, although you might have to negotiate a few contradictions. Straightahead Christians have to deal with the overt magic displayed in the *Life* and Columba's role as a *de facto* war god. Fans of cuddly Celtic Christianity might chose to ignore the curses shrivelling hands, striking people dead or sinking ships, and the general air of vindictiveness (in an unforgettable image, Stuart Airlie, in 'The View From Maastricht', describes saints like Columba and Adomnan as 'sombre Batman-like figures brooding over the communities entrusted to their protection, swift to avenge an insult to themselves or their followers.') The extreme, body-punishing austerity of the saint doesn't sit comfortably with contemporary culture ('The Celtic saints of modernity are all too often recognisable as the 'cushion saints' of the middle-class comfort-zone', Donald Meek, again). If you want an environmentally-friendly Columba, note that in the famous crane-caring story he does not care for the crane for its own sake, but because it comes from and is representative of his beloved Ireland; he slays a wild boar with just a word, and gives a man a magical stake on which animals are compelled to impale themselves. If your desire is for a neopagan, spiritually-inclusive 'Columba-as-Druid', watch out for all those unpalatable confrontations with pagans, usually consummated with classic Old Testament vengeance.

What is clear is that, even from shortly after their deaths, Columba and Adomnan were regarded as figures of great posthumous power. You could invoke them for aid and protection, but you also crossed them at your peril. And that lingering aura of awe, dread and power has shaped the way people have viewed Iona ever since.

2

LEGENDS AND FOLKORE

They have all of them a remarkable Propensity to whatever is marvellous and supernatural. Every Person has the traditional History of Columba, with numberless Legends...They are famous for the second Sight; full of Visions seen either by themselves or others; and have many wild and romantick notions concerning Religion and invisible things....They are a People, whose Imagination is evidently the most lively of all their Faculties. The huge Fabrick of artificial Superstition, erected on the Spot in which they live, has rendered the very Air of their Island infectious. Their un-limited Veneration for Antiquity, supplies the Place of Truth, in the most marvelous and frightfull Legends...

Revd Dr John Walker, on the Ionans, in
Report on the Hebrides of 1764 and 1771

For ourselves, we have tried to call spirits from all their reputed haunts, not only 'midst the deserted ruins of cathedral and nunnery, but likewise at the witching hour of midnight; we have visited many other haunts deemed by the vox populi 'far frae cannie' but in vain; 'spirit or goblin damned' alike disregarded our summons, and the 'good people', alias the fairies, have ever been (to us) invisible. Seeing is believing, we maintain; but, per contra, so also do the Ionians, almost all of whom have stories 'by the hundred' of personal encounters with the supernatural.

W. Maxwell, *Iona and the Ionians*, 1857

Iona is a treasure chest of myths, legends, folklore, beliefs, misconceptions and fictions. Some are generic – Maxwell records old women telling fortunes to local people by reading tea leaves. Others are much more Iona-centred. Where these are associated with a specific site – such as Reilig Odhráin, Sìthean Mòr or Columba's Bay – they are included in the appropriate chapter. Here I set out the various 'floating' stories that have no specific home other than just 'Iona'.

DRUIDS

The idea that Iona was a home to Druids is probably the most persistent of the stories associated with the island, despite the complete absence of evidence in its favour. This does not mean that there never were Druids here – Druids are known in Ireland up until the sixth century – but we have no documentary or archaeological back-up for their existence. All attempts to reconstruct Druidic pre-Columban Iona are therefore exercises in imagination, speculation or wish-fulfilment. Eighteenth-century antiquarians fell in love with Druids – or at least the idea of Druids – because they saw in these ancient sages a reflection of themselves. According to Roman writers the Druids they encountered in Gaul (France) and Anglesey were intellectual men of power. They were also magicians. For Georgian scholars it was an irresistible combination. Druids were (erroneously) supposed to have built Stonehenge and Avebury, and by extension every megalithic monument. By the mid-eighteenth century any gentleman of education 'knew' Druids had constructed every significant ancient monument in Britain. On Iona, Gaelic place names were shoehorned into 'Druid' translations. The standing stones on Mull were co-opted as markers for prehistoric pilgrims. Fiona Macleod published a series of mystical works which imaginatively reconstructed Druidic Iona; although little read now, their influence was huge and continues to shape the popular 'New Age' view of Iona as the Island of Druids. (To be fair, Macleod also mentioned that islanders in Lewis and Tiree used the word 'druid' in speech as a synonym for modern priests or ministers.) Swire identified Iona as the home of the magic cauldron of many Celtic myths, which cures wounds and resurrects the dead. The Old Irish *Life* says two bishops met Columba when he landed on Iona and demanded his submission, but it was revealed to the saint that they were false bishops and he expelled them. O'Donnell's *Life* improves this by making the bishops Druids in disguise. Both tales are of the 'Christianity overcomes pagans' moral-type. Sacheverell says Columba ordered all the Druids on Iona drowned when they refused to embrace Christianity. Logan (1831) has the Welsh carrying away the 'mystical instruments' from Iona when Columba suppressed the Druids, which enabled a Druidic revival to continue in Wales for several centuries. But there is no reliable authority for any of this. Neither Adomnan nor any other early chronicler speaks of Iona as held by the Druids.

WITCHCRAFT

A much-told story – repeated, for example, in *An Amazing Historical Account of the Belief in Witchcraft in Scotland* by Charles Kirkpatrick Sharp and in *The Darker Superstitions of Scotland* by Sir John Graham Dalyell, as well as by nineteenth- and twentieth century travellers' accounts – tells of how, in a time long before Columba, Natholocus, King of the Picts, sent a messenger to consult a witch who lived on Iona. A rebellion or war was looming and the king wished to obtain knowledge of the future. She consulted her familiar spirits and pronounced that the king would soon be murdered not by his open enemies but by a friend 'in whom he had such faith as to entrust him with a secret mission'. In other words, the messenger. The man swore he would see the witch executed before he would commit such a deed, but he brooded. If he told the king what the witch had said, he himself would be killed in anticipation. If he said nothing the king could hear it from someone else. So he did the only thing to save himself – he returned home and stabbed the king to death. The story can be traced to Hector Boece or Boethius (Pennant says 'Boethius gives us reason to suppose…Iona to have been the habitation of weird sisters and coco-daemons'). Boece's *Chronicles of Scotland* (1527) was hugely influential for centuries but has been shown to be ripe with fantasy and fictions: it is the source of many popular but erroneous beliefs about Scottish history. Other than the entirely fictional tale of Natholocus, there are no other reported accounts of witchcraft on the island.

FAIRIES

Iona has several stories featuring fairies, and many of these are told in the various geographical chapters that follow. In 1900 John Gregerson Campbell wrote in the *Superstitions of the Highlands and Islands of Scotland* that, 'There are old people still living in Iona who remember a man driving a nail into a bull that had fallen over a rock, to keep away the Fairies'. There may not be any connection, but one of the books written at the monastery in the ninth century, *The Canons of Adomnan*, contains a series of strange dietary prohibitions derived from the Book of Leviticus, including 'chickens that have tasted the blood of a man', and 'cattle that have fallen from a rock'. Campbell tells another tale of a man who was fishing in moonlight and fell asleep. He was awakened by a pull on his rod, so picked up his gear and his catch and headed home. A woman cried behind him, 'Ask news and you will get news'. The man realised she was an evil fairy and said, 'I put God between us', but this did not have the desired effect: the fairy attacked him and compelled him to meet her every night. To escape her he fled to the Lowlands and then America but she followed and killed him.

THE 360 CROSSES

Guidebooks endlessly recycle the unlikely story that 360 crosses were destroyed at the Reformation. Swire goes so far as to claim this number for the megaliths of a stone circle. J.R.N. MacPhail considered the evidence in a 1925 article called 'The Cleansing of I-colum-cille' and concluded the figure was a conflation of two remarks by Sacheverell (1688) – firstly, 300 stones with inscriptions had been noted, and secondly the Synod of Argyll ordered 60 crosses to be thrown into the sea. A relatively mild act against Popish monuments was indeed passed by the Synod, but they did not vigorously enforce it. In 1642 the Marquess of Argyll traipsed through the isles (including Iona) vandalising as much as he could, but the sheer number of crosses and cross-marked stones still on the island – which still bear the 'crucifixes, pictures of Christ and all other idolatrous pictures' supposedly banned by the Synod – and the fact that some of the largest free-standing crosses in Scotland remain in plain sight, belies the legend of wholesale destruction. In the absence of an expedition to drag the sea-bed for evidence, we can conclude the '360 crosses' story is a fiction.

MARY MAGDALENE

In *By Sundown Shores* Fiona MacLeod repeated a folk legend related to him by a man from Tiree. After the Crucifixion Mary Magdalene travelled the world with a blind companion; he loved her, but their relationship was celibate. They were on the run from Mary's first husband, a violent man, who eventually tracked them down to Knoidart. In desperation Mary hid the blind man among some pigs she was herding. But her husband, laughing, said, 'That is a fine boar you have there', and put a spear through the man. Then he cut off Mary's beautiful hair, and left. She died from a broken heart. Her body was found by one of Columba's monks. The saint knew who she was and commanded she be secretly buried in a cave on Iona. This is clearly a story – and a good story at that. Legends of Jesus, the Virgin Mary, Mary Magdalene or Joseph of Arimathea having visited a particular local area are told all over the world, from Glastonbury to Japan, and there are a number of these folktales recorded throughout the Hebrides. Over the years, however, some writers have made serious claims that Mary Magdalene, and Jesus, and their son, all lived on Iona for a while; in some versions the son is actually born on Iona. The preposterousness of this makes the Tiree boatman's tale – which brings together a biblical figure and a saint who lived five hundred years later – seem quite sensible by comparison

SNAKES

In Adomnan's Life Columba says, 'From this very moment poisonous reptiles shall in no way be able to hurt men or cattle in this island, so long as the inhabitants shall continue to observe the commandments of Christ'. Although here snakes are clearly just prevented from harming anyone, this passage has given rise to the notion that Columba actually banished snakes from Iona (possibly as a riposte to St Patrick, who expelled them from Ireland). There are indeed no snakes on Iona. An article in the Oban Times of 12 June 1920 by Revd J.G. Dawson Scott describes how 'Mr Ritchie' (presumably Alec Ritchie) on one occasion saw an adder swim onto the shore of Iona, wriggle onto the grass, then die. Seton Gordon, in Afoot in the Hebrides, mentions a snake being deliberately brought in a container onto the island only for it to die on arrival.

BARNACLE GEESE

Sacheverell was assured that large branches of fir were thrown up on the beaches with barnacle shells growing on them that contained the visible foetuses of geese. Movements could be discerned within the sacs. If kept out of water they would putrefy in a few days.

MERMAIDS

A maighdeann-mhàra (mermaid) fell in love with one of the monks, and each night she would pray she might be given a human heart and a human soul that her saintly lover might save for Christ. But her prayers were in vain and she was always compelled to return to the sea, weeping. As each of her tears were shed they turned to pebbles, and the small green marble stones known as The Mermaid's Tears are on the beaches to this day. This tale appears in several works, for example MacDonald Douglas' *The Scots Book*. A sixteenth-century carved bone disc found in the Abbey and now in the National Museum of Scotland shows a crowned mermaid holding a fish. Medieval depictions of mermaids, such as that on the Campbeltown Cross, often show them with a comb and mirror – and exactly the same female symbols can be found on many grave slabs originally from the Nunnery.

SEAL PEOPLE

The Hebrides are awash with tales of human-seal shape-shifters. St Patrick, when irritated, would turn unbelievers into seals. Columba was more temperate, preferring to convert gradually, but when he was away the younger monks on Iona would use the seal-curse through simple impatience. Swire writes that Christians who relapsed into paganism changed into seals, but that seals on Iona come together to sing for joy when one of them has attained salvation. This song is so pure, being the very music of Heaven, that no human can hear it and live. Alternatively, the song is a call or warning of death or an invitation to leave the land and join the seals. Fiona Macleod relates several stories (which, in Macleod's usual style, may be more fiction than folkloric recording). In *Iona* a seal called Domnhuil Dhu was heard laughing on the rocks below the ruined Abbey one Hallowe'en, telling the other creatures of the sea that God was dead. A man who heard him also laughed, and was instantly paralysed and fell into the sea. His body, when found, was 'beaten as with hammers and shredded as with sharp fangs'. In *The Sin-Eater* the an-cailleach-uisge (the siren or water-witch) inhabits the sea off Erraid. She is old and ugly but her voice and enchantments bewitch fisherman into thinking she is young and fair. She casts sea-spells and if the sailors mock the cailleach her two familiars, a black and a white seal, will upset the boat. A man netted one of those seals, but its companion attacked the trawl and boat with such ferocity that he had to cut the net adrift. A portion of the net snagged and was found to contain a tress of woman's hair. The cailleach is a complex mythform: in one of the stories she is both Lilith, Adam's first wife who left him to cohabit with demons, and Kirsteen McVurich, a nun seduced to the sea by the evil man-seal Angus MacOdrum, known as Black Angus.

Macleod's most fascinating tale, though, is of a fishing trip off Eilean Dubh, near Columba's Bay, and two miles from Soa, the seal island to the south. Two fishermen,

Ivor Macrae and Patrick Macrae, spotted a bull-seal on a rock. Instead of ignoring this common sight, Patrick stood up and launched into a Gaelic rosad or spell:

Ho, ro, O Ron dubh! O Ron dubh! An ainm an àthar, 's an Mhic, 's an Spioraid Naoimh, O Ron-à'-mhàra, O Ron dubh!

Ho, ro, O black Seal, O black Seal! In the name of the Father, And of the Son, And of the Holy Ghost, O Seal of the deep sea, O black Seal.

Hearken the thing that I say to thee, I, Phadric MacAlastair MhicCrae, Who dwell in a house on the Island, That you look on night and day from Soa! For I put rosad upon thee,

And upon the woman-seal that won thee, And the women-seal that are thine, And the young that thou hast, Ay, upon thee and all thy kin, I put rosad, O black seal, O Seal of the deep sea!

And may no harm come to me or mine, Or to any fishing or snaring that is of me, Or to any sailing by storm or dusk, Or when the moonshine fills the blind eyes of the dead, No harm to me or mine. From thee or thine!

Patrick then repeated the incantation, to be joined by Ivor. Macleod claims to have witnessed all this (which is now impossible to verify). Later, Patrick related the reason for the spell. His elder brother Murdoch was working as a shepherd on Bac-Mòr in the remote Treshnish Isles; he lived there alone and had no boat. On Hogmanay the Macraes' father, filled with sentiment and drink, sailed eleven miles from Iona to visit Murdoch, only to witness his son curse God, kill his collie, and slip into the sea with his new love, a seal. Murdoch became a danger to fishermen, who recognised his manic laugh as he tried to upset their boat. At midnight his voice was heard at the door of the family home, but Macrae senior would not let him in; in the morning he found his boat net destroyed. The following day, a Sunday, an exorcism expedition was mounted to Soa, where Neil Morrison the minister read extracts from the Bible to the basking seals, one of who was heard to laugh with Murdoch's voice.

SEA MONSTERS

'Uchd Ailiun', an old Irish poem falsely attributed to Columba, has the writer contemplating the joys of the ocean:

> *That I might see the sea monsters,*
> *The greatest of all wonders.*

(The poem is translated in full in Trenholme's *The Story of Iona*.)

Adomnan's *Life* tells how Saints Berach and Baithene each encountered 'a great whale' with jaws 'gaping full of teeth' between Iona and Tiree. Berach's sea voyage was disrupted by the creature but Baithene calmly blessed it and went on his way. What the beast was is impossible to say. Carmichael (*Carmina Gadelica*) collected the following Gaelic chant on Skye in the 1860s:

> *Seven herrings,*
>> *Feast of salmon,*
> *Seven salmon,*
>> *Feast of seal;*
> *Seven seals,*
>> *Feast of little whale of the ocean;*
> *Seven little whales of the ocean,*
>> *Feast of large whale of the ocean;*
> *Seven large whales of the ocean,*
>> *Feast of the cionarain-cro;*
> *Seven cionarain-cro,*
>> *Feast of great beast of the ocean.*

Carmichael identifies the cionarain-cro as the kraken, the largest of all sea serpents. So what does that imply for the 'great beast of the ocean'?

Swire (1964), describing the 'Things and People who knew Iona before the Saints set foot upon it', conjures up titanic Lovecraftian Sea-gods who used Iona as a feasting place on which to perform 'certain sacred rites…before man was known on earth at all' She also has the bones of a huge dragon being found here, 'proof' that the primeval Sea-gods sacrificed strange, massive creatures on the island. No remains of prehistoric animals or marine deities have been unearthed on Iona.

BEACH PEBBLES

Pebbles turn up everywhere. They are found in graves from the Early Christian period to the nineteenth century. They are marked with crosses and set up as grave markers. They are embedded in the floor of the Abbey Church, are piled on Tòrr an Aba, found on altars ancient and modern, are built into mounds by pilgrims, and mark impromptu pathside cairns. They protect from drowning and, when thrown back into the sea, symbolise the casting off of the dark things of the past. They are used for healing and for divination. They can be found at contemporary prayer spots and, at Columba's Bay, are shaped into modern designs. You'll probably end up taking some home.

3

THE VILLAGE

From the ferry pier the road splits into the three parts of the village: left for Martyrs Bay and the toilets and restaurant; right for most of the houses, the Argyll Hotel and the Bishop's House; and straight ahead for the Nunnery, Heritage Centre, St Columba Hotel and the Abbey.

SOUTH TO PORT NAM MAIRTEAR, 'MARTYRS BAY'

This is probably the place where Vikings killed sixty-eight monks in 806. But as with so much on Iona, the name Martyrs Bay may be a misnomer - mairtear is said to be a corruption of martira or martra, meaning relics. Just past the war memorial and west of the road at NM 285238 is An Eala★, a small mound, traditionally the place where the coffins of the illustrious dead were rested after landing. An Eala is a corruption of the Irish word for a coffin. The funeral parties would circle the mound three times *deisiol* ('sunwise') and take refreshments before proceeding along the Sraid nam Marbh, 'the Street of the Dead', to Reilig Odhráin graveyard. Sraid nam Marbh ran west-north-west from here to about 70m southwest of the Nunnery, then curved close to the present school as far as the heritage centre, and to just south of Maclean's Cross, where it joined the main road. Donaldson (1927) says where it turned to the right there was an old arch called *Dorus Tratha* ('time door'), although I can find no other references to this. By 1769 the first section of the road (to the Nunnery) had already disappeared. Local people still landed the remains of relatives at Martyrs Bay until at least 1848, preferring this site to the boat pier to the north. There are two 'Iona Boat Songs' in current circulation, both of them describing a kingly funeral party being rowed to the island (one goes 'Isle of Sleep where dreams are holy/Sails to thee a King who sleepeth/With thy Saints we leave him sleeping') but both are twentieth-century compositions and not ancient laments. In 1969 two burials by the mound were disturbed during the laying of a water main, so it was decided to excavate. The result was astonishing – forty burials were identified, many of them beneath the mound. Five were in stone-lined long cists but most had been placed without coffins in a central gully, packed together in a dense mass in which earlier burials were disturbed by later

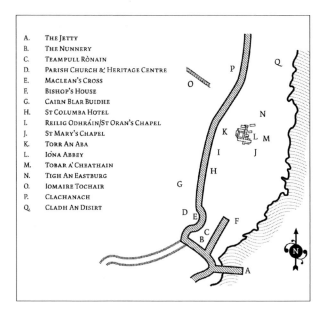

A.	THE JETTY
B.	THE NUNNERY
C.	TEAMPULL RÒNAIN
D.	PARISH CHURCH & HERITAGE CENTRE
E.	MACLEAN'S CROSS
F.	BISHOP'S HOUSE
G.	CAIRN BLAR BUIDHE
H.	ST COLUMBA HOTEL
I.	REILIG ODHRÁIN/ST ORAN'S CHAPEL
J.	ST MARY'S CHAPEL
K.	TORR AN ABA
L.	IÒNA ABBEY
M.	TOBAR A' CHEATHAIN
N.	TIGH AN EASTBURG
O.	IOMAIRE TOCHAIR
P.	CLACHANACH
Q.	CLADH AN DISIRT

Left: Map of the village.

Below: An Eala, where coffins were rested before being taken along the Street of the Dead to Reilig Odhráin. Below it were found dozens of graves.

ones. Some burials had been inserted into hollows in the adjacent rocks. Once this liminal area had ceased to be a burial ground blown sand built up and created the mound. In 1850 the Revd W. Lindsay Alexander described a place on the island called Clagh nam Martireach, the martyrs' cemetery; this may have been it. Of the individuals who could be identified, there was a weighting towards women with

an average age of forty. Neither they nor the fewer male bodies showed evidence
of hard labour or injuries due to violence, and of eight women examined none
had borne children. This grouping of celibate, high-status middle-aged women
strongly suggests this was where some of the nuns were buried, although there
was also a burial ground for women at the Nunnery itself. Alternatively, this was
where strangers to the island – and who did not have the status to be buried in
Reilig Odhráin - were buried. The earlier, encisted burials could have been any
period from the sixth to the tenth century. An inhumation accompanied by an
anvil stone of red granite was found "in the east end of Iona" in or before 1911.

Martyrs Bay is the site of the supposed house, now gone, of a folklore/real
world crossover figure called Pàraig an Oir, 'Peter of the Gold'. MacArthur
tells the well-known story, which comes in several different versions, in *Iona:
The Living Memory of a Crofting Community*. Peter was a fisherman, kidnapped
by a passing ship ostensibly to guide her through the treacherous rocks at the
south end of the Ross of Mull. Once in the open ocean he was held on board
and made to work without pay before being abandoned in America (or Spain).
Eventually other Highland sailors forced the captain to pay him a bag of gold
pieces as compensation and he went home with a dent in his shoulder from the
weight of the gold. His surname is variously given as MacArthur or MacInnes.
There was a real Peter MacArthur, who worked in the gold mines in Australia
for a year before returning to Iona in the mid-1850s to marry Mary MacDonald;
they emigrated to America in 1859. His descendants there have always called him
Peter the Gold. He may have been confused with the adventures of the fisherman or his own story elaborated.

NORTH TO THE BISHOP'S HOUSE

In 1802 The Hon. Sarah Murray (of Kensington) reported that, 'for ages no corpse
has been suffered without force to be carried out of the island; for as long as that
custom is maintained, say they, no Ionian can be drowned in the Sound between
I and Ross'. Ninety years later another traveller, Malcolm Ferguson, recounted a
related story he had been told by his local guide on Iona, although the root cause
had changed: corpses could not be taken from Iona because seven years of famine
would follow. The blacksmith, Rob MacLachlan, promised his dying mother he
would bury her in her native graveyard in Mull, no matter what the prohibition
against it. His plan was masterful. At the time the body was waked or 'watched'
for several nights before the funeral. The smith brought a liberal supply of whisky
to the wake and the young men gathered at the house were soon asleep. Rob's
friends made an opening in the thatched roof, hoisted the coffin out with ropes
and slid it to the ground; it was then loaded onto a boat in a sandy creek. Early
in the morning the older men arrived to relieve the youngsters. The smith met
them at the threshold and told them – much to their dismay – that they need not

trouble themselves further as his mother's body was twenty miles away on its way to her native parish. Note the smith had a number of friends to help so the custom could not have had universal approval. The date of this episode is uncertain but by the time Ferguson visited Iona (1893) the wake had been abolished for twenty years.

A spot at the north end of the village (NM 286241) was still in 1857 called Port a'chroisein, 'Port of the Little Cross', the site of Crois Adhamhnain, 'St Adomnan's Cross'. The placenames are now obsolete and the cross is lost, but what may be a fragment of it was found reused as a lintel in a house at the north end of the village; it is now in the parish church.

The Bishop's House has the only statue of St Columba on the island, erected in 1894 by an Episcopal bishop in the teeth of virulent opposition from the Presbyterians. Peter Underwood, in *Gazetteer of Scottish Ghosts,* tells the following story of his friend Tommy Frankland, a member of the Iona Community and former RAF officer. Tommy was with a group of students in the library of the Bishop's House one evening; an elderly ecclesiastic was standing by the open window, completely focused on something in the Sound of Iona. After a period he left the room, headed to the bay – and walked right into the water. He was up to his waist before Tommy reached the shore and shouted for him to come back, but it was some time before he actually responded to the entreaties. Afterwards he said he had seen the Abbey as it had been in an earlier age, and thought he would walk to it along the causeway. The causeway disappeared centuries ago. Until Tommy's shouts had finally penetrated his perception he had no idea he was in the sea. In the vestry of the chapel of the Bishop's House is a strange carved stone said to have been found on the site during the construction in 1890. On one surface is a triangular male face with one eye closed to a slit and the ears replaced by either horns or, more likely, some kind of headwear. It was probably an apprentice's trial piece.

MacArthur (1995) records two drownings with ritual consequences: two young MacDonald brothers when their boat was swept away in the 1880s, and two boys and a girl in 1908 when their dinghy capsized just off Eilean a' Charbaid, close to the end of the village. In each case the respective owners – Mr Kirkpatrick the schoolmaster and Angus MacPhail the postmaster – immediately destroyed their boats.

WEST AND NORTH TOWARDS THE NUNNERY AND ABBEY

On the opposite side of the road to the current phone box once stood the Clach a'Bhainne, 'the milk stone', a flat stone onto which milk was poured as an offering to the gruagach or fairy guardian spirit of the cattle. It is still there, below the tarmac. The ritual took place when the young women returned from tending the cows in the pasture. In the nineteenth century Alexander Carmichael saw several of this kind of 'leac gruagach' around the Hebrides.

The Nunnery: the Sheela-na-gig.

THE NUNNERY**

The Augustinian nuns arrived around 1200-1208, a part of the new way of religious life that was sweeping across Scotland at the time. The first prioress was Bethoc, the sister of Reginald, the Lord of the Isles who installed the Benedictine monks at the Abbey. Her tombstone, inscribed 'Behag daughter of Somerled son of Gilbride, prioress' survived until the early nineteenth century. The priory was dissolved around 1574. Although ruined it is one of the best-preserved medieval nunneries in the British Isles and, in its current be-gardened form, is an attractive, restful spot in good weather. In the early 1930s three propagated cuttings from the famous Glastonbury Thorn were planted in the garden – two succumbed to the weather but one survived until the 1960s when it was accidentally removed by a workman's spade. Sacheverell writes that deadly nightshade grew in the cloister garden, and was gathered by travellers for 'superstitious purposes'. Both Murray (1857) and Williams (1984) claim the ruins were haunted but I can find no account of a specific encounter and so conclude these stories belong to the 'creepy ruined building that must be haunted' category. A psychic told me that there were no ghosts on the site, but that that the nuns, led by 'Abbess Mary', were still present as higher spiritual beings who blessed all those who entered the ruins. Preservation work on the ruins in the 1920s unearthed four silver spoons and a broken gold fillet at the base of the chancel arch, probably hidden there in the thirteenth century; the items are now in the National Museum of Scotland in Edinburgh. Immediately south of the external main west window is a consecration cross, and there are several badly eroded carvings on the corbels: the south wall of the nave has a human head of indeterminate sex, an angel bearing a scroll, and the Annunciation.

Pride of place, however, must go to the exterior of the south wall of the refectory, facing the road from the pier, which has an eroded but still visible Sheela-na-gig. Sheelas are sexually-explicit female carvings found throughout the British Isles, with a preponderance in Ireland. The typical Sheela points to or openly displays her genitals, which may be over-exaggerated in pornographic detail. Not surprisingly these figures have been controversial since Victorian times and their placement on churches a source of embarrassment for conservative Christians and academics – even in recent times some museums have been reluctant to put the Sheelas in their collection on display, and it is quite common to find an architectural guide to a church which simply omits its Sheela altogether. Traditions associated with Sheelas show them to have been revered images (rubbing their genital area was an apotropaic act, thought to cure illness and provide protection) with great iconographic importance to the earlier church. This is shown by the Iona Sheela – she is probably in her original position, not hidden away, but in a very obvious location on a lintel above a window of the refectory. We are meant to see her. She is badly weathered but you can make out her squatting position and the way her arms reach down to her genitals, displayed between opened legs. The refectory was rebuilt in the late fifteenth century. For more detail on Sheelas I recommend McMahon and Roberts' *The Sheela-na-Gigs of Ireland and Britain.*

The Nunnery was used in medieval times for the burial of both nuns and lay-women of noble birth, and the tradition of burying women here instead of in Reilig Odhráin continued until the mid-eighteenth century. There is a row of grave slabs to the east of the ruins. Other stones from here are in the museums at the Abbey and Teampull Rònain.

TEAMPULL RÒNAIN (ST RONAN'S CHURCH)*

NM 285241. Standing next to the Nunnery, this twelfth/thirteenth-century building was formerly the parish church for the ordinary people of the island in medieval times, and is now a sculpture museum. It is built on the site of an eighth-century church and an even earlier Early Christian cemetery. The more recent burial ground adjoining is Claodh Rònain, St Ronan's churchyard. After the building became ruinous in the post-reformation years a large number of burials took place in the church, with a clustering around the former altar. The burials were all of women or young children, and this seems to have been an exclusively female cemetery. Reeves (1874) recorded the names of nine burial grounds on the island, and these names seem to preserve an early medieval practice of burying the dead in the different locations according to gender and status – women/men, noble, craftsmen, unbaptised infants and criminals, and so on. McNeill in *The Silver Bough* describes healing stones being kept on the altar. A number of the graves contained small water-rolled pebbles of white quartz, up to fifteen in one case. Deposition of these white stones is known in burials in Ireland and the western Scottish seaboard from the sixth to the twentieth centuries. Stone circle fans will be reminded of the scattering of white quartz 'godstones' found in many prehistoric megalithic sites. A hoard of thirteenth-century gold objects – a fillet, a small fragment of wire and a ring – was found during excavations and is in the National Museum of Scotland. A row of grave slabs lies outside the north wall. There were two St Ronans. The one commemorated here is probably the eighth-century Abbot of St Blane's monastery on Bute.

The museum is usually locked; for access ask permission at the Abbey. Note the stones are not actually on display, more in storage in horizontal racks, so it can be very difficult to see details. The numbers in brackets are the identifying numbers ascribed by the RCAHMS in *Argyll 4*. 'RO' means the stone was formerly in Reilig Odhráin; 'N' means it came from the Nunnery. The stones include:

(177) (N)   Late fifteenth-century, broken in two. In the upper panel are two elaborately dressed two laywomen in niches, with below them two nuns under canopies, with a mirror and comb. The lowest panel is upside down, with a priest standing beside an altar with a chalice, and a kneeling attendant.

(107)   Discovered in the south choir aisle of the Abbey in 1875, dated *c.* 1500-1509. Two men in armour under a double canopy. Below, galley with spread sail and foliated cross. Inscription: 'Here lies John MacIan, lord of Ardnamurchan; and Mariota MacIan, his sister, wife of Malcolm MacDuffie, lord of Dunevin in Colonsay, bought this stone for her brother'.

(178) (N)   Two canopied niches with a laywoman (left) and a nun (right). Barely legible inscription: 'Here lies Mariota, daughter of John, son of Lachlan, lord of Coll, and…on whose souls God have mercy'. Mariota is the laywoman, the nun may be her sister. *c.* 1500-1560.

(184) (RO)   In the top panel is a broken-off cloaked figure with a staff (often called the pilgrim); in the lower panel plant scrolls issue from the tails of a pair of dragons. Fourteenth-fifteenth century.

(193)   Fragments of a slab, with a foliated cross, and a claymore flanked by plant scrolls from the tail of a griffin (left) and an indeterminate animal to the right. *c.* 1500-1560. Traditionally ascribed to Maclean of Gruline.

(181) (RO)   Fourteenth/fifteenth-century slab with two confronted wolf-like creatures above a sword.

MACLEAN'S CROSS**

NM 285242. This striking late fifteenth-century monument at the side of the road is thought to have been commissioned by the Clan Maclean as a wayside prayer cross, but earlier authorities thought there was no direct connection with the Macleans and the 1857 introduction to Reeve's edition of Adomnan's *Life* says 'Its name is plainly a vulgar misnomer'. The 3.15m high cross stands at what was the junction of three medieval streets but there is a tradition (noted in the Ritchies' *Iona Past and Present*) that it once lay recumbent in the Nunnery grounds. The present pedestal does appear more modern than cross itself. Perhaps the cross is in its original position but was re-erected after lying broken in the Nunnery for a time? Marsden (1995) suggests Maclean's Cross is on the site of a much earlier cross raised to mark the death on that spot of Ernan, Columba's uncle, a holy man who Adomnan records dying a short distance from the harbour. The central disc has Christ on the cross; on the reverse there are two opposed beasts just below the disc; the inscription on the bottom panel, along with a mounted warrior, has eroded away. In the 1850s an islander saw Eoghan a' chin bhig (Ewan of the Little Head) pass him here, riding a black horse and carrying his diminutive noggin under his arm. (source: MacMillan & Brydell, *Iona*, 1898). At a savage clan battle on Mull around 1538 Ewan MacLean's horse bolted with its master's recently decapitated body still in the saddle, and careered around the island for several days. Ewan's supposed grave slab is in the Abbey Museum. He is one of Mull's best-known ghosts; sight of the horse and headless rider presages a misfortune for the Macleans of Lochbuie.

PARISH CHURCH

NM 284242. This plain eighteenth-century church is close to the site of the vanished Cill Chainnich and Cladh Chainnich, the Chapel and Burial Ground of St Kenneth. Kenneth, who died in 599 or 600, was a friend and comrade of Columba. He accompanied him on his visit to the Pictish king Brude, near Inverness; when the pagan ruler threatened them Kenneth paralyzed Brude's sword-arm with a prayer. Adomnan tells of a miracle/case of second sight/ telepathy involving the two saints. Columba and some companions were about to capsize while sailing in a storm. Columba told the others not to be afraid, because, 'God will listen to Kenneth, who is now running to church with one shoe to pray for us'. At that very moment, back on dry land, Kenneth jumped up from the table and rushed off, half-shod, to the church, to pray for the safety of his friends. The boat, of course, made landfall safely. The foundations of the graveyard were removed some years before 1857, in which year only a few tombstones remained. Three very worn stones lie in the grounds. Inside is a fragment of a late medieval cross-shaft with an armed man holding a spear,

Blàr Buidhe prehistoric burial cairn.

found in one of the houses in the north of the village. This may be St Adomnan's Cross, although no positive identification is now possible.

BLÀR BUIDHE CAIRN*

NM 284243. This is the only confirmed prehistoric ritual or funerary monu-ment on the island. It can be found 60m west of St Columba Hotel, behind the St Columba Arts and Crafts Steadings. It was (poorly) excavated in 1875; no evidence of the burial was found. Only two of the large boulders of the kerb are *in situ*; five others lie nearby. The 1m x 0.3m stone in the southeast corner is not shown in the plan of the 1875 excavation, and may therefore be a recent addition. The cairn was formerly called Tigh Finn, Finn's House. Many ancient monuments are associated with the mythological hero Finn (Fingal), but here the place-name may be suggestive. Blàr Buidhe means 'yellow field' but it is also the name of an Irish giant. The tale of how Fingal had no power of sitting down or rising up when in the giant's house was still circulating orally on the west coast in the nineteenth century. Reeves (1857) reported Crois Bhriannain, 'St Brandon's Cross' near Tobar Orain ('Oran's Well') just east of the Free Church manse, now the St Columba Hotel, and Alec Ritchie (1928) notes Parc nan Croisean just south of the hotel. All have vanished.

4

REILIG ODHRÁIN AND ST ORAN'S CHAPEL

REILIG ODHRÁIN **

The name means 'Oran's Graveyard'. It was the burial ground of kings and chiefs, the terminus of 'The Street of the Dead', and a place of sanctuary in medieval times. Dr Johnson called it 'this awful ground', in the sense of awe-full. And at its heart is the mysterious, clouded figure of Oran, one of the more legend-haunted names of Dark Ages Iona, all the more so because so much is told of him and so little can be proved.

The legend is first written down in the Old Irish *Life of Columba*, dating from the tenth century, and exists in several later variants. In the earliest form, Columba said to his monks, 'It is well for us that our roots should go underground here…It is permitted to you that some one of you go under the earth of this island to consecrate it'. Oran immediately volunteered, saying, 'If thou wouldst accept me, I am ready for that'. And thus, almost casually, begins a most un-Christian tale of human sacrifice. Columba said, 'O Oran you shall receive the reward of this: no request shall be granted to anyone at my tomb, unless he first ask of thee' and Oran was duly interred alive. Three days later, wanting to see the face of his dear companion one more time, Columba ordered the grave to be opened. To the shock of all, Oran opened his eyes and exclaimed, 'There is no such great wonder in death, nor is Hell what it has been described'. (The word for Hell used in the original is Ifrinn, or Ifurin, the Gaelic Hell, the Land of Eternal Cold.) At this, Columba straightway cried, 'Uir, Uir, air sùil Odhráin! mun labhair e tuille comhraidh' – 'Earth, earth on Oran's eyes, lest he gossip further' – and the living dead Oran was covered up again.

Later variants on the tale give the reason for the sacrifice. Each night the building work of the monastery was thrown down by unknown supernatural forces. Men posted on watch were found dead in the morning. Columba determined to find the cause and himself stayed up all night on guard. At midnight he was visited by a terrifying sea-spirit, half woman, half fish, which told him, 'I do not know what casts the stones of your walls to the earth, nor what takes the lives of your brothers, but it will continue to be so until you have made the proper sac-

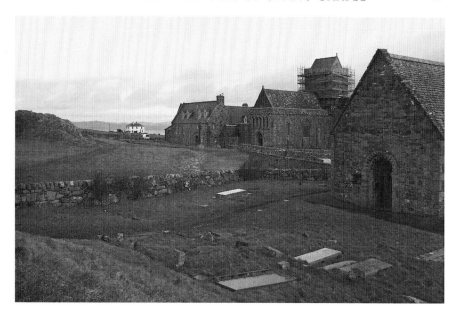

A ritual landscape: graveyard, mortuary chapel, Street of the Dead, High Crosses, Abbey Church, holy well and site of founder's cell.

rifices'. The proper sacrifice, of course, being a live burial. Once Oran had been sacrificed, the building of the church proceeded undisturbed. In another version, Columba and Oran had a profound disagreement about the nature of Heaven, Hell and the fate of the dead, so Oran had himself buried alive to prove his contention. Sacheverell, writing of this 'comical story' in 1688 says the reason Oran was buried was to alleviate a great famine afflicting the northern parts of Britain. Oran offered himself provided Columba would build a chapel in his name. Oran was buried standing upright, and the grave was opened after twenty-four hours, whereupon Oran 'began to entertain Columbus and his company with so particular an account of the state of the dead, that the good man did not think it safe to trust him any longer among the living...and sent him to the other world, where he had already made so good an acquaintance'.

Various themes can be teased out of this extraordinary tale. On the one hand, it is an example of the widespread folkloric motif of the 'can't be built church', in which the holy building cannot be erected in one spot because it displeases the fairies, or the Devil, or another supernatural entity. Either the church has to be moved to another spot or the demonic force is overcome in some appropriately Christian manner. In addition, some writers have linked Oran's volunteering to die with the Celtic-Druidic practice of the willing sacrifice. Several Iron Age 'bog bodies' found in the British Isles were high status victims who had lived a good, indeed luxurious life before their (presumably willing) death, and may have been given a narcotic before they were ritually executed (an excellent example can be found in Ross and Robins's *The Life and Death of a Druid Prince*). Here, as in the Oran tale, the idea is to propitiate the spirits of the land or water. Oran is described as Columba's cousin; and Columba was of royal blood. So we have a high status, willing sacrifice who dies to placate the denizens of the Underworld: the story may be a distant echo of a genuine sacrifice during Druidic times, in another location, and grafted on to the 'celebrity' of Columba. People returning from the dead are common in Celtic folklore and, of course, resurrection 'after three days' is central to the story of Christ. In addition, Jesus and several saints – including Adomnan and, on several occasions, Columba – raised people from the dead. The strangest element, given its Christian setting, is Oran's description of death and hell, which is not only blasphemous but sits uncomfortably with the Columban proselytising mission. If you want to push the Jesus-Oran analogy further, you could see Oran's burial and resurrection as a pagan listener's garbled version of the story of Jesus (the willing sacrifice who returns after three days dead and whose message is, essentially, to not fear death or hell).

The Oran story continues to fascinate and be elaborated. A mid-twentieth-century guide to the Abbey, *Come Around With Me* (priced 1s 6d) by the Revd George Macleod, founder of the Iona Community, claims Oran as the last of the Druids. In an overwrought mystical play, *Odrun: The Rune of the Depths* (1928) Eleanor Merry, a follower of Rudolf Steiner, has Oran as the reincarnation of various initiates from ancient Greece to first-century Druidic Iona, eternally compelled to attempt to communicate with the Great Mysteries. Merry expands this in tortuous (and, to my mind, incomprehensible) detail in *The Flaming Door*, in which Oran is somehow implicated in the control of the chthonic magnetic forces that shape our world, our collective sub-conscious, and all world religions. In a 1997 article (*Odhran: Patron Saint of the Lower World*) Frank MacEowen has Oran insist that his grave is built deep enough for him to walk around in, with a stone roof. When, after twenty days (not three) the roof is removed, Oran is still walking round in his 9ft grave; he leaps out and goes into panegyrics about the wonders he has seen under the earth and in the world of death. MacEowen also notes some people see Oran as a kind of shamanic patron saint, an Orpheus-like figure who travelled to the Underworld and returned with occult knowledge.

To find out anything approaching the truth of the Oran story is difficult. Certainly Adomnan does not mention either Oran or the legend, and Oran is not one of Columba's original twelve companions listed in Adomnan's *Life*. So we can dismiss the idea that Oran was with Columba on Iona. There does appear to have been a historical Oran, but his story is confused. St Oran of Latteragh in County Tipperary, Ireland is supposed to have founded some kind of Christian sanctuary on Iona before dying of plague in 548 or 549, fifteen years before Columba arrived on the island. There is no reliable evidence for this: the foundation may have been elsewhere. Oran also appears in placenames on

The Street of the Dead.

Tiree, Colonsay and Mull. This Oran is described as an Abbot, so he could not have been on Iona with Columba. A later tradition has Oran evicting two false bishops from Iona, denouncing them as Druids and burning their books, which seems to be the same story as Columba's (see Legends and Folklore chapter). Adomnan (*Life*) describes Columba visiting an unnamed monk, a Briton, and therefore a foreigner, who was dying from 'a bodily affliction'. When the old man died Columba saw angels and demons in the air fighting over his soul, with the angels carrying off *'the first among us who has died in this island'* (my emphasis). This experience Columba related to Aidan, Liber's son, a monk, but told him not to reveal this in Columba's lifetime. In a note to the 1922 edition of the *Life,* the editors, A.O. and M.O. Anderson say, 'This chapter differs greatly from the legend of the death of Odran in the Irish *Life of Columba* [as described above] and it may have been written on purpose to contradict an early form of that legend'. Thomas Hannan, in *Iona: And Some Satellites* (1929) suggests this unnamed Briton was confused with both the historical Abbot Oran and with the Gaelic objection to the first burial in a cemetery: the spirit of the dead person is required to watch over the graveyard. In some versions the watcher is always the most recently buried, but in others it is the first, there forever. Hannan gives an example known to him (presumably from the 1920s) where the council graveyard overlooking a sea-loch somewhere, which replaced an ancient burial ground, was avoided for years before an incomer was buried there. There is an occasionally repeated story (e.g. in Spence, 1905 and Swire, 1964) that the 1560 Synod of Argyll, in the white heat of the Reformation, destroyed a stone circle on Iona because the people continued to worship in it. When the circle was raised each of the twelve inner stones had covered a man buried alive. Later the monks cut the sign of the cross on the stones and carved them into the freestanding crosses still visible today. The Revd George Macleod's guidebook, *Come Around With Me,* says there was a Druid Circle where the Abbey Church now stands, and shows an illustration of six tall straight megaliths supporting a hexagon of Stonehenge-type trilithons. Even the doyenne of archaeological stone circle studies Aubrey Burl mistakenly refers to a destroyed stone circle to the west of the Abbey. It all originates with Sir Godfrey Higgins' ludicrous *The Celtic Druids,* published in 1827. Higgins was a member of the fantasy/revivalist Order of Druids and his work is typical of the times – the Druids came from India, built Stonehenge, and evolved into Christian Culdees. The tale seems to be a confusion of several different elements, filtered through a lens of Romantic Druidry: pagan monuments were certainly Christianised in the Dark Ages; stone circles were destroyed elsewhere from the sixteenth century on but there is no evidence of a stone circle having been on Iona, Pennant's uncertain description of a cairn on Sithean Mòr notwithstanding; the Synod did meet on the island (but in 1642) to pass a relatively mild resolution against idolatrous monuments (by which it meant explicitly Roman Catholic monuments, usually featuring the Virgin Mary or figures of saints); and the 'buried alive' element is presumably an echo of Oran.

At what point the principal graveyard next to the Abbey became named after Oran is not known, but it was at least by the late eleventh century. An addition of that date to the eighth-century document called the kalendar or Martyrology of Oengus gives Oran's feast day as 27 October and calls him 'Odran of Relicc Odran in Iona of Colum Cille', and a Middle Irish poem from the same late eleventh-century period gives the same description. The poem also mentions the belief that Columba sanctified the graveyard with soil brought from Rome – an erroneous tradition still current in the eighteenth century (source: RCAHMS, *Argyll* Vol 4). Clearly the name Reilig Odhráin references the idea that Oran was the first to die and be buried here. Fiona Macleod, writing in the 1890s, said some local people regarded Oran's grave as an oath-site, on a par with the Black Stones, and Martin claimed Oran was buried in St Oran's Chapel, but I can find no reference elsewhere to a specific grave identified as Oran's. Reilig Odhráin itself has gone through many changes. The existing boundaries (except on the north) have only been in place since the eighteenth and nineteenth centuries – the original cemetery may have extended much more to the east. The site was probably the original monastic graveyard, which was separated from the monastery itself by a 3m deep ditch, a symbolic and actual distinction between the living and the dead, the clean and the unclean. A Viking cremation in a boat-shaped grave was found on the bank of the Vallum near the graveyard. This was clearly a pagan rite, but its location may suggest the Norsemen wanted to tap into the power of the site.

At some point Reilig Odhráin became the preferred burial place for the illustrious dead of Scotland. How and when this happened is not clear: it was probably due to a combination of several factors: magical – the proximity to the primal power of Columba; soul-saving – Iona's soil was so sacred it would expunge even royal sins; fashion – in the seventh to ninth centuries several kings and princes had retired from political life to become monks on Iona, and had been buried there; prestige – an Iona burial was the ultimate status symbol, the Hebridean equivalent of Westminster Abbey; territorial – demonstrating an ancestral and future commitment to Gaeldom/the Isles/Alban; and prophetic – Iona would survive the end of the world. The prophecy comes in several variants but its basic form is:

> *Seven years before the Judgement,*
> *The sea shall sweep over Erin at one tide,*
> *And over blue-green Islay;*
> *But the Island of Columba*
> *Shall swim above the flood.*

Just who among the illustrious dead was buried here is now impossible to say. So much has been written, but so little proved. In 1549 Dean Munro provided the first written report of Reilig Odhráin, describing three stone tombs like little chapels. The largest, in the centre, was inscribed *Tumulus Regum Scotiae* and contained the remains of forty-eight Scottish kings. To the south was a tomb marked *Tumulus Regum Hiberniae*, in which were held four Irish kings; and to the north the *Tumulus Regum Norwegiae* covered eight Norwegian kings. There was also a French king buried nearby. The inscriptions were clearly still extant, but we cannot judge how reliable this report is – note Munro did not actually see any individual bodies or graves, and the inscriptions gave no names. So either someone on the island told him the numbers, or he based them on chronicles and king-lists then available. The tombs were probably mortuary chapels, possibly of twelfth century date. By Martin's visit (1695) the inscriptions had vanished. Walker (1764) said only the central structure was still (just about) standing, the other two shrines having been reduced to grassy heaps. In 1772 Pennant recorded only the slightest of remains. It is therefore now impossible to determine which if any of the supposed monarchs and princes were actually interred in Reilig Odhráin. The French king may have fared better – a pink granite grave slab incised with a plain Celtic cross with a bottom tenon, held in the Abbey Museum, is said to be his. Angus Lamont, one of the nine-teenth-century guides on the island, said he was a French prince who died while visiting a 'Lord MacDonald' and had requested burial on Iona.

The lack of documentary or archaeological proof, however, has not stopped people with an interest in this sort of thing attempting to compile a 'death list' for the sixty Scottish, Norwegian and Irish monarchs, although modern his-torians have largely seen this as a fool's errand. Candidates for the Norwegian king-list have pushed the meaning of both 'king' and 'Norwegian': they have included Somerled, the first Lord of the Isles (d.1164); Godred, sub-king of the Isle of Man (d.1187); Haco-Huspac, king of the Sodorian Isles (d.1228); and Olaf, king of Dublin, who died on pilgrimage in Iona. The Irish contingent may number Neil Frasach or Pluviosus, who reigned as king of all Ireland for seven years before retiring to Iona where he was buried in 778; Artghal, son of Cathail, king of Connaught, who died on Iona in 791 after eight years spent in seclusion; and Cormac MacAird. All these claims should be treated with cau-tion, even dismissal, as should Martin's recording of a stone seen not by him but by the Minister of Jura, who claimed it commemorated an Archbishop of Canterbury.

The Scottish list of forty-eight kings is probably the most contentious, as some candidates are legendary rather than reliably documented individuals, the king-lists and chronicles have been manipulated and changed by later scribes for propaganda and dynastic purposes, and the very number itself is suspect. One of the most common claims includes the entire House of Alpin, from Kenneth MacAlpin, first King of Picts and Scots (d.860) to Macbeth (d.1057) and his step-son Lulach. Shakespeare famously mentions Duncan, the king murdered (at least in the play) by Macbeth:

ROSS: *Where is Duncan's body?*
MACDUFF: *Carried to Colmekill / The sacred storehouse of his predecessors / And guard-ian of their bones.*

Macbeth Act II Scene 4

There is now no way to determine if Duncan, Macbeth or any of the dynasty are actually buried here. Many writers see the burial of Malcolm Canmore (Malcolm III, d.1093) in Dunfermline Abbey, not Iona, as a symbolic act: the break con-firmed that the political focus – and destiny – of both the Alpin dynasty and the Scots nation had moved from the ancestral, Dalriadic west coast to the main-land, and from Gaeldom to the English-speaking Lowlands. The establishment by Somerled of the defiantly Hebridean Lordship of the Isles in the mid-twelfth century reinvigorated the tradition, and for generations the Lords and their kins-men were buried in Reilig Odhráin, as were the chiefs of other clans. This is

probably the period when the coffins were rested on An Eala before proceeding along the Street of the Dead. The chiefs buried here include MacDonalds,
MacLeods, MacKenzies and MacLeans. The practice declined after the forfeiture
of the Lordship of the Isles in 1493.

William Collins (1721-1759), in *An Ode on the Popular Superstitions of the
Highlands of Scotland, Considered as the Subject of Poetry*, imagines these mighty men
now holding a parliament of the ghosts in Reilig Odhráin:

> *… at midnight's solemn hour,*
> *The rifted mounds their yawning cells unfold,*
> *And forth the monarchs stalk with sov'reign pow'r,*
> *In pageant robes, and wreath'd with sheeny gold,*
> *And on their twilight tombs aerial council hold.*

It is not just the three monarchial mausolea that have been lost: many grave
slabs have been relocated, first to St Oran's Chapel and then to the Abbey and
Nunnery Museums or the Abbey; others have vanished. There has been a great
deal of disturbance, and it is no longer possible to tell where any of the graveslabs
were originally located. Some medieval stones – including that of the 'Four
Priors' (now in the Nave of the Abbey Church) – were effectively regarded as
private property; the belief was that even the most sinful could get into heaven
in the slipstream of a saint, and so up until the mid-nineteenth century some
islanders were buried under a holy man's grave slab. Then came the antiquarians, digging up and cavalierly redistributing slabs. In 1858 the finest stones were
arranged in two railed enclosures – the 'Ridge of the Kings' and the 'Ridge of
the Chiefs' so beloved by Victorian visitors – although the choices were purely
arbitrary and the identification of individual monuments dubious. A great deal
of semi-learned speculative energy was expended on the stones with Old Irish
inscriptions, which even produced a parody in reaction, William Combe's 1821
The Tour of Doctor Prosody in Search of the Antique and Picturesque, in which a group
of eager antiquarians find evidence in Reilig Odhráin for the entirely mythical
Ossian. Alec Ritchie clearly enjoyed guiding visitors around the ruins but probably got fed up with being asked for the location of Macbeth's grave. MacArthur
(1995) relates how, when one visitor complained that the previous year the graves
of Macbeth and Duncan had been closer together, Ritchie replied that they had
had to be separated because the two ghosts quarrelled so much. He also claimed
that, winters being long and a bit dull on Iona, the islanders took to shifting the
grave slabs around to deliberately fox the next season's visitors. And finally, there
was a troop of sacred monkeys living over the hill. Also buried in Reilig Odhráin
is Netta Fornario (see Sìthean Mòr); look for the small open book marked
'M.E.F Aged 33 19 Nov. 1929', just to the north of the northwest corner of St
Oran's Chapel.

St Oran's Chapel. A psychic told the author that St Oran, a Learned Master, still inhabited the building.

ST ORAN'S CHAPEL **

This plain oblong building is the oldest upstanding structure on the island, being probably twelfth century, although some parts may be 200 years earlier. It was probably built by Somerled, the first Lord of the Isles (d.1164), or by his son Reginald. The tradition that the saintly Queen Margaret (d.1093) built the chapel seems unsupported. MacArthur (1995) sensibly suggests that Margaret's alleged reconstruction of the monastery did not take place, and the single medieval reference to it was designed to boost her reputation for her daughter's husband, Henry I of England. The chapel was used as the mausoleum of the MacDonalds, Lords of the Isles. It was restored in 1957 after remaining roofless for three centuries. The twelfth-century west doorway had sixteen animal or human heads but these are now very worn. In the south wall is an elaborate late fifteenth-century tomb recess with two lion springers. The first order has two horned fabulous beasts and, at the apex, a Green Man. Martin (1695) described the Green Man as arms of the MacKinnon family, 'a boar's head, with a couple of sheep's bones in its jaws'. In the second order are three human heads (one with a bishop's mitre). At the very top is a Crucifixion. The carvings are very worn so you will need a torch to see them. The name of the tomb's occupant is not known for certain, although it may have been intended for John, the last Lord of the Isles (d.1503). Six grave slabs, two of them decorated, are set into or lie on the floor. Five other grave slabs line the north wall – RCAHMS numbers 131, 174, 126, 152 and 157, all of which appear to have had a long association with the chapel. The fourteenth- to early sixteenth-century number 152 has a galley with furled sail and a banner or possibly a carved figurehead on the stern post, with, below, two pairs of opposed beasts. Number 157, of a fourteenth- to fifteenth-century date, has a foliated cross and a hound pursuing a stag. To the right of the elaborate sword is a griffin, to the left, a lion and dog. The clach-bràth, the Day of Judgement Stone, once stood just outside the chapel (see the Abbey Museum).

5

THE ABBEY COMPLEX

The accretion of later monuments presents Iona as a ritual place. This can be seen in two main trajectories; one is the amplification of the primary monastic site by its satellite churches and cemeteries; the other is the specific focus of several monuments around the tiny chapel known as St Columba's Shrine.

Jerry O'Sullivan, *Iona: archaeological investigations, 1875-1996*

…nothing escaped Destruction, but those parts of the Buildings, and such solid Monuments, as were proof against the Hands of Rage, and even the Teeth of devouring Time.

Revd Dr John Walker, *Report on the Hebrides of 1764 and 1771*

The buildings that can be seen today are mostly the twentieth-century restorations of the thirteenth-century Benedictine Abbey which became ruinous following the Reformation. With the exception of the vallum (boundary wall) and Tòrr an Aba nothing can be seen of the Columban monastery that existed here from 563 to around 1203. As shown by excavation, the wooden huts and church of the original monastery founded by Columba lie underneath the current Abbot's House, refectory, cloisters and the west part of the Abbey Church. Further wooden buildings existed in the small field between the Abbey and Reilig Odhráin and between Tòrr an Aba and the Abbey. After several rounds of destruction by Viking raids the monastery was rebuilt in stone only to suffer further raids in 986. Despite these setbacks the Columban monastery did continue. But somewhere around 1200-1204 the Irish monks were ousted by members of the Benedictine Order, the change being instituted by Reginald, son of Somerled, the first Lord of the Isles. This was one of the many examples of the suppression of the Irish/Celtic tradition and its replacement by the new, Europeanised political-religious hegemony being established throughout Gaelic Scotland. An entry in the Irish Annals of 1203 states that, 'A monastery was erected by Cellach without any legal right, and in despite of the family of Iona…The clergy of the North (of Ireland) assembled to pass over to Iona…and in obedience to the law of the Church, they subsequently pulled down the monastery'. What was actually going on in this bizarre episode is uncertain, but the date given is around the time Reginald installed the

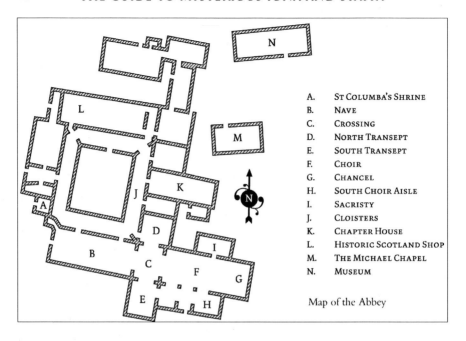

A. St Columba's Shrine
B. Nave
C. Crossing
D. North Transept
E. South Transept
F. Choir
G. Chancel
H. South Choir Aisle
I. Sacristy
J. Cloisters
K. Chapter House
L. Historic Scotland Shop
M. The Michael Chapel
N. Museum

Map of the Abbey

Benedictine monks at the Abbey, and there may have been a dispute with some of the ecclesiastics already established on Iona. Note that the Cellach referred to is not Abbot Celach, as the latter was on Iona in the early ninth century. No more is heard of this curious attempted coup. The Benedictines immediately began constructing the grand Abbey which forms the blueprint of what we see today and which was built over the Columban monastery. It is therefore convenient to think of the various structures, stones and carvings still visible as being divided into two broad periods – Early Christian (pre-1200) and medieval (post-1200), although for much of the eleventh century Iona was essentially Norwegian territory and there are two Scandinavian monuments as well. The Abbey complex was expanded and changed over the centuries until, as part of the next great upheaval in religious life – the Reformation – it was dissolved in the late sixteenth century. Thereafter the Abbey was effectively owned by the Maclean Clan of Duart until the Campbell Dukes of Argyll acquired it by force in the late eighteenth century. A short-lived attempt at restoration in the 1630s amounted to very little and the state of the buildings worsened. In 1875 some consolidation and repairs took place. In 1899 the eighth Duke of Argyll, who owned the entire island, transferred Iona's historic monuments to the Iona Cathedral Trust, who started the restoration process that continued through the twentieth century, much of it after 1938 under the auspices of the Iona Community. Some of the buildings around the cloister are still used by the Community and not open to visitors. In 2000 the Cathedral Trust passed guardianship of the Abbey, Reilig Odhráin, St Ronan's Church and the Nunnery to Historic Scotland.

MAGICAL THINKING

The Abbey complex is a prime example of the way a site and its associated elements can become a focus of magical thinking, even among overtly pious Christian populations. The key node here is Columba; it is his power, his protective magical aura, that people have wanted to tap into for more than 1400 years. His original tomb may have been in what is now called St Columba's Shrine – and numerous graves were later dug as close as possible to the Shrine. In medieval times pilgrims flocked to visit Columba's enshrined bones in the Abbey Church – again a focus of burials, often high status ones. Kings and chiefs fought to be buried in Reilig Odhráin as the proximity of Columba and his saints meant the sacred soil would wash away their sins and ensure an entry to heaven. On 19 January 825 St Blathmac was martyred in the newly-built stone monastery. The Vikings first used torture to try to make him reveal the location of Columba's portable shrine with its precious metals, but Blathmac had remained purposely ignorant of where the other monks had buried it, and so died. The account suggests that his killers studied his entrails in an attempt to divine the whereabouts of the shrine. Blathmac was a 'suicide monk' – he had deliberately gone to Iona at the time of Viking raids to die for Christ. His remains were enshrined at the monastery and became the focus of miracles. Up until 1756, when the practice was abolished by Neil Macleod, the new minister of the parish of Kilfinichen and Kilvickeon, islanders would carry a corpse around the whole of the ruined Abbey complex before burial. Cross-marked pebbles were used as gravemarkers in imitation of Columba's stone pillow. Fragments of the medieval marble altar had an apotropaic function, as did other carved stones. Rainwater collected in some Abbey stones brought favorable winds to sailors. Other stones were used for divination, or for swearing oaths, or for apocalyptic purposes. A mid-twentieth century guide to the Abbey, *Come Around With Me,* states, 'modern mystics claim the beneficent vibrations are stronger here than anywhere else in the whole fabric of buildings'. The sheer amount of behaviours and activities based on magical thinking is breathtaking.

THE VALLUM*

This earthwork formed the boundary of the monastic precincts, and remains to an impressive height west of the road. Aerial photography and excavation has shown that the vallum is complex and built over more than one period, although the mightiest surprise came from an excavation in 1988: a radiocarbon date for the peaty topsoil beneath the bank returned a date of first or second century AD, several hundred years before Columba arrived. What was here before and who was building it? This riddle remains unresolved. (Source: Jerry O'Sullivan, *Iona: archaeological investigations, 1875-1996.*)

TÒRR AN ABA**

Probably the best place to start is this rocky hillock, 'the hill of the Abbot', which has a superb view of the Abbey. This may have been the site of Columba's writing cell. Swire (1964) tells the story of two jackdaws, rescued by Columba from a storm, acting as the saint's watchdogs around his cell; the jackdaws who lived in the ruins before reconstruction were supposedly descended from this pair, and, having been blessed by the saint, would always have the same size of population. The guidebook *Come Around With Me* describes the scene with imaginative detail and the eye of faith: the bluish stones just to the south were the walls of Columba's Hut, the slanting gray rock was his couch, what looks like an open-air fireplace was his seat, with a wooden board across the two stone ends, and on the inlaid stone base below, he kept his pigments. Tòrr an Aba is probably the hill on which Adomnan reports Columba blessing the monastery and assembled monks on his final day, and prophesying Iona's future fame: 'Unto this place, small and mean though it be, great homage shall yet be paid, not only by the kings and peoples of the Scots, but by the rulers of barbarous and distant nations with their people. Thy saints also, of other churches, shall regard it with no common reverence'. There is a medieval cross-base on top, surrounded by quantities of beach pebbles, presumably placed there as an act of veneration by pilgrims. Martin describes the hillock as 'Dun Ni Manich, *i.e.*, Monks' Fort, built of stone and lime, in form of a bastion, pretty high'. There is no evidence of any fortification, but excavation in 1956-7 found the remains of a large stone revetment which could have increased the usable space at the top. The area with flowers and seats between Tòrr an Aba and the south range was pointed out to Victorian visitors as 'St Columba's Cell' and later was called 'the Old Guest House' but it is in fact the monastic bakehouse and brewhouse.

ST MARTIN'S CROSS***

This eighth or ninth-century freestanding cross, 21m west of the Abbey Church, is one of the most impressive examples of Early Christian carving. The shaft of the east face has numerous serpents and spirals and, above the central roundel, two sets of leonine beasts. On the lower part of the west face twelve snakes writhe around six bosses. Snakes are symbolic of the Resurrection. Above are four biblical scenes: four indeterminate figures, probably David and Goliath and David with Saul; David playing a harp and a musician with a triple pipe – the box between them may be a drum or a book, probably the psalms; Abraham about to sacrifice Isaac, with, to the left, the angel looking on; and Daniel between two lions, with a possible third lion's head to the right. Each side-arm of the cross has a lion and the top arm has three pairs of lions with intertwined tails, all protecting the Virgin Mary and Child with four angels in the central roundel. Alec and

The replica of St John's Cross throws its shadow onto St Columba's Shrine. The tiny oratory is the *omphalos* or fulcrum of the entire Abbey complex.

Euphemia Ritchie in *Iona Past and Present* state that in 1927 Prof RAS Macalister had the bottom panel on the east side freed from lichen and discovered a faint inscription in Irish letters: 'A prayer for Gilla Christ who made this cross'. They also mention that a bronze spoon was found in the socket under the shaft when the cross was restored upright, apparently in the nineteenth century. It is possible this is confusion with St John's Cross. The spoon was sent to Inveraray, by which I think they mean the Duke of Argyll. St Martin (316-400) established monasticism in Gaul. There is an unfounded tradition that Columba visited the tomb of St Martin at Tours.

ST JOHN'S CROSS***

This magnificent cross, probably the most impressive single monument on Iona, stands just in front of 'St Columba's Shrine'. It is a concrete replica of the original, which has fallen several times, the fragments being in the Abbey Museum. In the lowest panel of the east face the spiral and bosses motif is combined with two roundels formed by snakes, some fiercely biting other snakes or lizards. Other forms of snake-and-boss ornament are seen on both faces of the shaft and arms. The constrictions of the arms are filled with interlace in which are grouped small zoomorphic figures. Above the end-moulding of the top arm is a damaged finial which on the east face shows two confronted beasts and on the west face appears to include two wrestling figures. The west face also has 'hidden' crosses – saltires and an upright cross.

'ST COLUMBA'S SHRINE' **

There is a group of monuments which seems to focus very clearly on the heart of Iona's ritual landscape: St Columba's Shrine… their final grouping indicates a long-established and clear focus on the site now occupied by the mortuary chapel.

Jerry O'Sullivan, *Iona: archaeological investigations, 1875-1996*

Although the footings of what has for centuries been called St Columba's Shrine are ninth or tenth century, everything else is a twentieth century best-guess restoration of what it might have looked like. Columba's actual ninth-century shrine was elsewhere, in the principal church of the newly stone-built monastery. It is however possible that this tiny building, perhaps an Early Christian oratory, was indeed the site of the saint's original tomb, a tradition current since at least Martin (1695). In Adomnan's lifetime the tomb was still regularly visited by angels and illuminated by heavenly light. Skene (1877) relates a story of fertility magic from the eleventh century *Life of St Cadroë*. His mother could not have children so she and her husband passed the night in prayer and fasting at Columba's grave. They received a vision of themselves holding two candles which merged, and a man in shining clothes foretold how their son would be a future light of the church. Cadroë was born *c.* 900. Magnus Barelegs, King of Norway, visited Iona with his army in the late eleventh century, having already plundered the Isles, putting many to the sword. As related in the *Orkneyinga Saga*, he opened the door of the oratory but, such was the sense of awe associated with this place of primal saintly power, he did not go in but locked the door and declared no man should be so bold as to enter. When William the Conqueror ordered the body of St Cuthbert – another saint of powerful Christian magic - to be exhumed in Durham in 1072, he was immediately struck with an intense fever which caused him to flee. Perhaps Magnus decided that, tough warrior though he was, was still not about to offend a famously vengeful saint. The 'Shrine' was originally freestanding and was only joined to the church buildings as late as the fifteenth century. This separation from the medieval church – and even the location and orientation of the Abbey Church – may have been a mark of respect for the building's sanctity. Beneath the current wooden floor are two stone cists, each 2m by 0.5m. For centuries visitors were told the southern was Columba's and the other that of his successor Baithene or his attendant Diormit, although the cists are probably both late medieval, several hundred years too young. Other medieval burials crowded around this locus of saintly power and after the Reformation the area next to the Shrine became a private burial aisle. However, by the early nineteenth century the area, despite being still identified as Columba's shrine, was just a clearance heap. Built into the anta (stone projection) south of the door is a moulded fragment, probably from the ridge of a mortuary house such as those formerly in Reilig Odhráin.

THE BLACK STONES

Somewhere in the area of the Shrine may have been An Leac Dhubh, 'the Black Stone' (or Stones) of Iona, one of the most mysterious of all the lost supernatural relics on the island. The Stone was binding on an oath, although traditions vary – either the Stone would turn black if the person was lying, or the perjurer himself would turn black, or his reputation would be forever black, or there would be further occult retribution at a later date. Martin (1695) described how 'MacDonald, King of the Isles, delivered the rights of their lands to his vassals in the isles and continent, with uplifted hands and bended knees, on the black stones'. McNeill in *Iona: A History of the Island* notes that, 'As recently as the reign of James VI and I, two clans foreswore a long-standing blood feud and pledged themselves to friendship by the Black Stones'. Their description varies greatly between different accounts. Martin says they were kept a little to the west of Torr an Aba but later accounts have them as being next to St Martin's Cross or, usually, close to the 'Shrine'. Angus Lamont, the nineteenth-century local guide, placed the location at the entrance to the cloisters. There was one Stone, or several – although it is possible the original had become fragmented. Around 1365 John MacDonald, the Lord of the Isles, was captured by Lachlan and Hector MacLean and taken to Iona where on the Black Stone he was forced to pardon the MacLean brothers' recent murder of the MacKinnon chief. John also had to grant his daughter's hand and the lands of Duart in Mull to Lachlan, and Lochbuie in Mull to Hector. The Stone was usually described as grey, whereas Fitzroy MacLean's version of the story in *West Highland Tales* has John seated on a block of black basalt (Maclean, however, admits himself that his are storyteller's tales and not historically accurate). An old legendary trope has the Stone being the biblical Jacob's Pillow, which was brought from the Holy Land via Egypt and Ireland to Iona. Columba crowned Aidan King of Dalriada on it, it moved to Dunstaffnage and was thence taken to Scone where it was known as the famous Stone of Destiny. Edward I translated the Stone to Westminster Abbey where it remained under the Coronation Chair until being returned to Scotland in 1996. Of all the stories associated with the Black Stone this is the silliest, whereas the most likely is that the Stone was a carved tombstone of a late medieval type. Several early accounts make this identification – Pococke (1760) was shown a broken ecclesiastical figure, and later accounts (for example, MacLean's 1845 *The Native Steam-boat Companion* and MacMillan and Brydall's 1898 *Iona: Its History, Antiquities etc.*) also describe a human or priestly figure on a slab, although these were based on hearsay, as the Stone was destroyed by a local religious fanatic

The Cradle of the North Wind/
pilgrims' foot-washing trough. Note
the faint Greek equal-armed cross at
the end.

around 1820 or 1821. A letter in the *Oban Times* of 22 July 1932 by 'Druid' says
the date was 1817. The letter mentions a sketch book made at Iona by Sir William
Gell (1777-1836) in 1798 or 1801, which contains a small drawing of the stone
'by which the Chiefs swore'. The sketch apparently resembles the usual description of the stone as 5ft high with a figure of a priest in high relief. Boece briefly
mentions a reliable pagan oracle stone on the island and Martin describes another
stone which granted skill in steering a ship if the arm was stretched over it three
times in the name of the Trinity. The identity of this stone has never been established – it is entirely possible it is one of the stones in the Abbey Museum.

Like so much else conjectured about Iona, it makes a good story.
F. Marion McNeill, *Iona: A History of the Island*

THE ABBEY CHURCH – EXTERIOR***

The trough outside the church door was used by pilgrims to wash their feet. The
stone was also known as 'the cradle of the north wind', as blowing on its water
in the appropriate manner could magic up a favourable wind (see also Tobair
na Gaoithe Tuath). It may be one of the stone fonts between the Abbey and the
Nunnery noted by MacArthur (1990): if emptied of rainwater by a virgin they
would ensure a fair wind for sailing. In 1938 the Duke of Argyll refused to allow the
newly-established Iona Community access to a water supply outside the Abbey

Dragon, west front.   *Tau* cross, south wall of nave.

Crocodilian dragon, south wall of nave.

precincts. What happened next, as described by MacArthur (1995), reached near-miracle status within the Community's own internal mythology. Water diviners were brought in but could find nothing; on their last day their steamer was late and in that hour they discovered a good source, in the rubble just outside the west door of the church. To the locals this was just silly, as they had used the well for generations. It may be the 'St Columba's Well' from which Boswell and Dr Johnson drank. Once thought to be Early Christian, it has been shown by excavation to be of a sixteenth-century date. The parapet (built in 1875) makes a good place to sit to study the west front. For many years it was claimed that the wide foundation surrounding the well was the base of a tall Irish-type round tower; excavation in 1979 showed the tower 'foundations' to be just late medieval paving. The pink granite stone with three depressions, broken into two and placed around the well, is a former grinding stone from the bakehouse or a mill on the nearby stream.

Here is a tour of the external carvings on the Abbey Church. *West front*: a small severely-eroded figure at the apex of the door; on one of the corbels above, a twentieth-century dragonesque monster. *Nave* (south side): another modern dragon and a T-shaped *tau* cross on the corbels (the *tau* cross is interesting: T was once the last letter of the Greek alphabet and still is of the Hebrew, and Middle English works often substituted 'Alpha and Tau' for 'Alpha and Omega', although

Right: The font in the nave. Snake-and-boss ornament, knotwork, and the Cross.

Opposite: Griffin, graveslab of Prior Cristinus MacGillescoil, in the nave.

this particular cross may be that of St Anthony of Egypt, the father of Christian monasticism – perhaps the dragon is a reference to the devils with which he was famously tormented in the desert); west window, a man with a bird of prey and a crowned queen with a book and, at her throat, an equal-armed cross; main window, three men who are probably all representations of St Columba – the one at the top has a crozier and dove and is identified by the letters SC, the left man holds a crozier and ship, and on the right the figure holds a beehive and gives a blessing; single east window, an eroded head. *South transept:* west wall, third corbel from north, badly eroded head(?); south window, a girl praying, a boy singing and the Paschal lamb. *South choir-aisle:* grotesque face at the apex of the east window. *Chancel:* south wall, seventh corbel from east, badly eroded carving (tail of a fish?); three weathered figures on each of the south, east and north windows. *Tower:* each of the four angles of the corbel-course of the parapet has an animal head, and carved human heads can be seen on the east window; immediately below is a seated figure, very weathered. If you look really closely on the church fabric you will find three masons' marks in the form of individual letters.

THE ABBEY CHURCH – INTERIOR***

The early thirteenth-century church would have been a dark, forbidding place; it was enlarged and made lighter in the fifteenth century to accommodate the large number of pilgrims. The architectural history of the interior is both fascinating and complex: here, however, we are concentrating on the more curious elements, both carved and otherwise.

THE NAVE***

Six grave slabs rest against the south wall. The numbers refer to the identifying RCAHMS labels above them.

(205)   A mid-fifteenth century slab brought back to Iona in the nineteenth century from Kilvickeon, Mull, where it was taken after the Reformation. The inscription reads, 'Here lies Brother Cristinus MacGillescoil, sometime Prior of Iona, on whose soul may God have mercy'. In the top left is a griffin with spread wings. Several griffins (or gryphons) can be found on other grave slabs. On a warrior's monument they probably denote ferocity. Here, the symbolism is Christian: the griffin incorporates the symbols for the evangelists Mark (the body and paws of a lion) and John (the head and wings of an eagle) and, by complex association also comes to stand for both the bread and wine of the Eucharist. The vegetation spreading from the griffin's tail includes a circular object which may be the host, and the tail skims the surface of the chalice.

(201)   An Abbot with a staff making the sign of the blessing.

The nave. The crosses mark burials and the pebbles were found in the graves.

(199)   Formerly in Reilig Odhráin. Below the effigy of an Abbot two hooded
         figures greet one another, perhaps St Paul and St Anthony, the founders
         of monasticism, or simply monks – thirteenth to fourteenth century.

(200)   The Four Priors' gravestone. A hound pursuing a hare above four panels
         of florid carving. The inscription round the edge reads, 'Here lie four
         priors of Y, of one tribe; viz, John, Eugene, Patrick, formerly a bachelor
         in divinity, and another Eugene, who died in the year of the Lord 1500'.

(137)   Formerly in Reilig Odhráin. A priest (praying) and an attendant before
         a draped altar with a chalice and a ring headed cross. Could the sword
         below suggest a warrior who became a monk?

(179)   Nothing easily visible.

Next to them is a replica of the Book of Kells, which was almost certainly com-
menced in Iona and completed in Ireland. Up until the nineteenth century it was
called 'St Columba's Book', supposedly written in his own hand (and was presented to Queen Victoria as such) but it postdates Columba's death by around 200
years. The modern font, a masterpiece by Peter Macgregor Chalmers (1859-1922)
is richly carved with Christian symbolism: the Trinity (three fish); Eucharistic
sacrifice (Paschal lamb and banner); resurrection (cross); and Holy Spirit (dove
exhaling breath to humankind). Below the main panels are smaller symbols: a
Greek cross; a chi-rho monogram (the letters chi and rho form the abbreviated
Greek word for Christ); HIS, the abbreviated form of Jesus; and Alpha and Omega,

The nave, north wall, first window
from west: cross in a temple.

The nave, north wall, fourth window from west: the unusual Alpha.

the first and last letters of the Greek alphabet: 'I am Alpha and Omega, the first and the last' (*Book of Revelations* 1:11). The Alpha symbol is unconventional, lacking the cross-bar and being more akin to a mason's mark than an A. Exactly the same pair of symbols are found on the north wall. Elsewhere on the font there is Celtic ornamentation: the tongues of paired serpents extend into interlace; two dogs intertwine and give rise to interlace, as do a pair of peacocks; snakes interlace in corners; a cross is subtly formed out of curves and bosses. To the north of the main entrance a doorway marked 'Stand Fast' leads to a small chamber huddled in the low northwest watch-tower. Donaldson (1927) describes the folklore of this room. It was the 'Tailor's Hole', where the monks kept the tailor who made their habits. They made him work so hard he suffered terrible visions at night, including a fleshless hand that appeared in the wall saying 'Take a great grey paw that is without meat!' Fixed on a ledge by the modern stair is a broken cresset-stone – it looks like a prehistoric cup-marked rock but was actually used for lighted wicks floating in oil in the hollows. During the 1910 restoration eleven burials were found: six are marked by small crosses on the floor of the lower nave down the steps. The two groups of small pebbles embedded in the floor were found near the heads of two of the graves. Perhaps each pebble represents the age of the deceased? Or the number of mourners at the funeral?

There are many modern carvings in the nave. *West wall:* southernmost window, two confronted lions whose tails turn into the interlaced foliage above them.

The crossing. A soul in torment or a focus for the voice so the minister is heard throughout the church?

South wall: third corbel from west, Celtic cross in radiance; eighth corbel from west, crown; second window from west – west side, cow's head nestling in interlace, east side, wyvern with gaping jaws, coiled body and pointed tail. *North wall*: first window from west, two lions attacking a tree (probably based on an image in the Book of Kells in which lions consume grapes from the vine which emanates from Jesus), and a cross revealed by doors thrown open from an arcaded shrine; eighth corbel from west, a saint, in a niche, holding a figure of the boy Jesus above the waves; fourth window from west, two sets of interlace, one with the sign for Alpha and the other for Omega, duplicates of the symbols found on the font.

THE CROSSING***

Here you will find a superb and strange collection of carvings. Many are eroded, so a torch will help to bring out the full details. *Northwest corner*: the Temptation of Adam and Eve, with the Serpent coiled around the Tree. *Northeast corner*: two fabulous beasts without forelimbs, entwined with foliage. *Southwest corner*: a man carrying a beam with a pan at each end; he holds a circular object above one pan, while a second man crouches by it. It may represent a proverb.

The North Transept. Figure of a king with broken-off jaw on west side of rose window.

Southeast corner: Adam and Eve covering their nakedness in the Garden, confronted by the Angel of the Expulsion carrying a sword; a man with a leash around a huge beast (dog? lion? monster?); a hound twisted back on itself so it can bite the head of a bird on its tail; two wyverns, their bodies becoming foliage; an inscription, +DONALDUS O [BROL/CHAN F] ECIT HOC OPUS, 'Donald Ó Brolchán made this work', the name of the fifteenth century master-mason; a bearded lion-like monster with one head and two bodies, the tails becoming foliage; two winged dragon-like creatures, one swallowing a fish, the other its own tail; the sacrifice of a cow, with one man holding its tail, a second forcing down the head for it to be struck by a third man with an axe, and a priest(?) praying – this may have had a Eucharistic significance, with the cow representing the body of Christ (or does the scene represent the theft of the cow, the 'priest' being the goodwife wailing and the man at the right being the owner about to tackle the thieves?); a dog pursuing a hare (above the cow-killing scene); two bearded human-headed monsters wearing caps, with looped tails turning into foliage. There is a mason's mark in the rough shape of an hourglass below head height on the south face of the pillar.

On the east face of the west arch is a superb carving of a man with a staring expression and a mouth open in a shout or scream; his cap may indicate he was one of the masons working on the fifteenth century rebuilding.

NORTH TRANSEPT**

The central arch of the east wall had a statue, possibly of St Columba, but only the feet survive. A secret passage used to run along the east side in the thickness of the wall, leading to the tower, possibly a site of refuge.

The oak screen with the carvings of the four Evangelists – Winged Man (Matthew), Lion (Mark), Bull (Luke), Eagle (John) – was gifted by the Queen. Nestling in the decoration between the figures are a sea-serpent, dragon, gryphon and another monster, all interlaced and biting each other's tails. The carvings are based on images in the Book of Kells.

The huge rose window on the north wall was added during the early twentieth -century restoration as a piece of artistic licence based on nothing more than the architect's whim. Heavily criticised both then and since, it has been excluded from the official architectural history of the building and is usually in darkness, so it's very hard to see the carvings – you will need a very powerful torch. On the east is a mustachioed man with closed eyes wearing an ecclesiastic's hat. The west side has coiled dragons and a crowned long-haired king with closed eyes. His beard and jaw have fallen off, making him look like he has a gaping mouth the width of his head.

Chancel, south window: cat-headed monster.

Chancel, south window: monkey.

Chancel. The modern altar, replacement for the original destroyed by seekers after talismanic protection against drowning.

Chancel. The winged figure of the Evangelist Matthew tucked into the mitre of Abbot John MacKinnon.

SOUTH TRANSEPT*

East wall: circular consecration cross. These crosses marked places for the bishop to anoint with oil during the ceremony of consecrating the church. The white marble table-tomb of the eighth Duke of Argyll (1823-1900) was installed in 1912; the matching sculpture of his third wife Ina was completed by the same sculptor some time before her death in 1925.

THE CHOIR***

There are more superb carvings here, on the south choir-arcade:

West column: a bishop in a niche; the Crucifixion with the Virgin Mary and St John in attitudes of grief – the cone may be the Hill of Calvary; the Virgin and Child attended by two angels, one with a harp; a man striking another with a sword (possibly Peter cutting off Malchus's ear or Cain killing Abel); a long-haired figure with a staff and a 'wild man' appearance, possibly John the Baptist; a man with a sword, perhaps John's executioner; an amazing Weighing of Souls, in which a winged St Michael, holding a balance with a human head on each pan, struggles against a four-limbed, clawed demon whose bottom is being pecked by an ibis.

East column: two entwined lion-like creatures without forelegs; a four-legged beast biting on a sprig of foliage; a winged, four-legged griffon with an ibis-like bird in its beak; a foot-soldier with an axe and an armoured horseman with a spear.

The doorway to the sacristy (on the north side of the choir) has corbels with crouching Atlas figures and a seated lion, and there is a very weathered head above the central columns. Also, set into the floor of the choir is a heavily worn four-teenth- to fifteenth- century grave slab with a small armoured figure and a pair of opposed animals from whose legs and tails develop intertwined plant scrolls.

THE CHANCEL AND HIGH ALTAR***

The communion table is a modern replacement for the original, annihilated in an apotropaic frenzy. In 1688 Sacheverell saw the white marble altar almost complete, 1.8m long and 1.2m broad. In 1749 John Campbell said 'it was much broke at the corner, by the Country People, who imagine it to be a relict of St Colm and conclude it an Antidote for any disease in Man or Beast, and especially the flux'. Shipwreck, fire, miscarriage and other misfortunes soon were added to the list and when Pennant visited in 1772 only a small part remained, which he and his party 'contrived to diminish'. In 1773 Dr Johnson described it as destroyed. A piece was preserved at the Andersonian Institution of Glasgow in 1800 but this cannot now be identified by the Institution's inheritors, the Hunterian Museum and Strathclyde

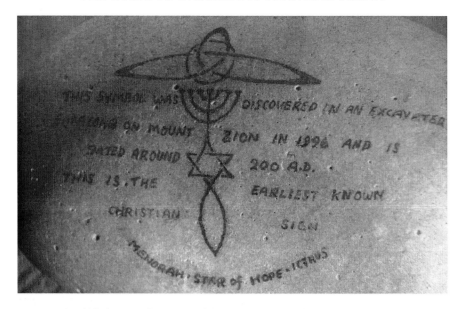

Decorated pebble kept in the recess of the east window of the south choir-aisle.

University. In 1864 the sole remaining fragment, some 0.88m square, was taken to St Andrew's Episcopal Church, Glasgow, where it became the consecration slab for the altar, 'Safe', as the Red J.F.S. Gordon wrote in his *Ecclesiastical Chronicle for Scotland,* 'from the digits of Moth and Thief'. The piece was transferred in 1975 to St James's Episcopal Church in Springburn, Glasgow, where it still resides. The legs of the modern altar are extensively carved with Christian symbolism (crosses, Alpha and Omega, HIS, chi-rho, Paschal lamb) and vegetation and Celtic knotwork. The modern cross on the altar echoes St John's and has a model of a reliquary on the top.

Sea spleenwort ferns grow on the walls, probably having taken root when the Abbey was roofless. In the south wall the triple-seated sedilia, where the priests sat, has several carved human heads, some with bishops' mitres. The canopy above the recess has two angels drawing back a curtain. Two headless angels support the bowl of the damaged piscina where the vessels of the Mass were washed, possibly including an ancient gold chalice looted from the Abbey after the Reformation by the Macleans of Duart. Sir Lachlan Maclean, fearing an invasion by the Duke of Argyll, asked his friend Aeneas of Glengarry (Lord Macdonnell and Arross) for military assistance, and celebrated the alliance with a drink from the chalice. Glengarry was horrified – 'I came here to defend you against mortal enemies, but since by sacrilege and profanation you have made God your enemy, no human means can save you'. Glengarry left Maclean to face the invasion alone and took the chalice. Eventually it made its way via various bishops to St Mary's Roman Catholic Chapel, Calton, Glasgow, from where it was stolen in 1845 and melted down (source: Daniel Wilson, *Prehistoric Annals of Scotland* and *The Scotsman* 8 January 1894).

The southern of the two full-length effigies is probably Dominic, son of Gille Coinnich, Abbot 1421-*c.*1465. The pillow is supported by angels, now headless. At the feet were two crouching lions, of which one survives. The other sculpture is the heavily vandalised and restored effigy of Abbot John MacKinnon, raised on four lions (only one original) and with now headless angels supporting the pillow. A scroll identifies one of the angels as Gabriel. Three of the four Evangelists are represented: the scroll is held by an eagle (John) and on the other angel are the two clawed feet of the lion (Mark), while in the fold of the mitre is a winged human figure (Matthew). There is no sign of Luke's bull. The inscription reads, 'Here lies John MacFingone, Abbot of Y, who died in the year of Our Lord 15--, on whose soul may the most high God have mercy, amen'. The date was left incomplete. He clearly expected to live to 1500, but died two years before. On the floor is a marble slab commemorating a MacLean, portrayed as a burly knight in armour; its hollow matrix once held a brass, long since stolen. Both Sacheverell and Walker were told the metal was actually silver, a belief disproved when a fragment of the brass was presented to the Iona Community by an anonymous visitor in 1966; nothing is known about how this relic was acquired.

West door of nave into cloisters: foliaceous beasts flank the symbol of Christ.

The cloisters. Lazarus.

The cloisters. Grave slab number 149 with horseman, hound and harper.

The best thing in the Chancel is a curious twinned carving on the south window: a crouching monkey and a creature with a cat's head atop the body of a wyvern.

SOUTH CHOIR-AISLE*

A headless lion attacking a bird on the south capital of the east window. In the window recess, two cross-marked stones (numbers 9 and 38). Small crosses on the floor mark more graves found during the restoration.

THE TOWER

In 1875 faint carvings of the instruments of the Passion (the hammer and nails, the ladder, spear, sponge, column and scourge) were identified on the central shaft of the south window of the bell chamber of the tower. They have now faded away completely. The tower is not open to visitors.

THE CLOISTERS***

Two doors open off the nave into the cloisters. The cloister side of the west door has modern carvings: two lions flanking a chi-rho; two foliate spiralling monsters creating a HIS; and other foliate beasts.

With the exception of two surviving medieval examples, all the arcade capitals of the cloisters were carved between 1968 and 1998. Most were completed by Chris Hall, except eight by Douglas Bissett. For in-depth detail on the carvings' symbolic meanings and biblical references, and Chris Hall's thoughts on the creative and spiritual aspects of his work – as well as great photography – I recommend Ewan Mathers' superb book *The Cloisters of Iona Abbey,* from which I take the names of the carvings.

Southeast corner: Baptism
> South cloister walk, moving east to west – Birds of Iona: gannet, osprey, snipe, heron, dove, merlin and swallow, great northern diver, corncrake, tern.

Southwest corner: Raising of Lazarus and Nativity.
> West cloister walk, moving south to north – Plants of the British Isles: primrose, medieval 1 and 2, dog rose and heather, bog myrtle, Christmas rose, lily of the valley, spring gentian, snowdrop, birdsfoot trefoil, honeysuckle, butterwort, warren crocus, sundew.

Northwest corner: Breaking of Bread and Offering of Wine.
> North cloister walk, moving west to east – Plants of Iona: marguerite, ivyleaf toadflax, thistle, Scottish rose, dandelion, navelwort, foxglove, iris, harebell, tormentil, sea campion, saxifrage.

Northeast corner: Alpha and Omega, and Parable of the Mustard Seed.
>   East cloister walk, moving north to south – plants of the Holy Land: thorns,
>   oak, darnel, narcissus, cyclamen, bulrushes, vine, wheat, vetch, palm, the
>   Burning Bush, olive, fig, anemone.

In the southeast corner of the cloister garth can be seen the northwest part of a small stone building which may be the church of the tenth-century stone-built monastery. A mass burial, presumably of Celtic monks, was found against its walls. MacArthur (1995) tells how Ian Cowie, a member of the Iona Community, watched as the archaeologists exposed the skeletons of seven or eight men who had died violently, one with his pinkie clamped between his teeth. The comment of Ian's young son on the grisly sight was, 'I suppose that's what you call a skul-lery!' MacArthur speculates they were the victims of the Viking raid of 986. The bodies were re-buried in the Abbey grounds. A badly worn head looks down on the scene from the apex of the window on the west wall of the north transept, above the cloister roof.

In the north cloister-walk, the entrance to the present refectory stair has a whitewashed lintel which is a cross-marked Early Christian slab, inserted in 1875. In the northwest corner is the undercroft doorway, rebuilt in the late fifteenth century at an oblique angle and now the entrance to the gift shop. On its east lintel is a grotesque bearded face with thick lips and gaping mouth. Next to this is the original refectory doorway, now blocked and ruined. Face grave slab 191 which is mounted in the recess, and look left – virtually invisible in the space that has been cut into the wall to show the previous arch head is a small crouching animal with bulbous eyes. You will need a torch. The bearded carving was done when this creature was concealed by later masonry – both figures were perhaps intended to warn those entering against gluttony. Another head, now featureless, sits on the east side of the two-arch arcade inside the Chapter House, off the east cloister, where you can also find a circular carpet with the same classical labyrinth design that is constructed from beach pebbles at Columba's Bay.

Arranged around the cloister is a magnificent collection of grave slabs com-memorating leading West Highland families including the MacDonalds, MacLeods, MacKinnons and MacLeans. Not all the slabs are described here – just the ones with the most interesting carvings. Note that this arrangement may change, so you may find some of the slabs elsewhere. The numbers are those found in the labels above the stones. As elsewhere, I recommend a torch. Many of the stones have had several homes, so where known the slab's provenance is shown, as this often provides crucial context. 'RO' means the stone was formerly in Reilig Odhráin; 'N' means it came from the Nunnery; 'SO' stones were recorded in St Oran's Chapel. All the slabs are from the fourteenth-fifteenth century except where noted.

Anti-clockwise from the entrance through the pend on the west cloister:

(118) (RO)   Plant scrolls on the left side of the cross shaft spring from the tails of dragon-like animals.

(155) (RO)   Foliated cross, galley with furled sail, illegible inscription, asymmetrical interlace surmounted by two pairs of animals, a stag attacked by hounds.

(159) (RO)   Man in armour on horseback with spear, casket, niched figure of a kneeling woman holding a rosary(?). Sword flanked by plant scrolls from the tails of two animals.

(153) (RO)   Very elaborate foliated cross at top. Galley with furled sails and animal figureheads on stem and stern posts. To the right of the galley is a hound pursuing another animal. Intertwined plant scrolls spring from the tails of two sets of opposed animals. The third from the left is winged. Traditionally the stone of Ailean nan Sop, Allan of the Straw or Brand, Allan Maclean of Duart, a notorious pirate, murderer and burner of homes who died in 1551.

(163) (N)   Foliated cross, rest of decoration of encircled foliaceous motifs issue from the tails of a wyvern, a lion and a manticore, a monster with a bearded human head.

(151)   Galley with furled sails and banners or figureheads at stem and stern. Three animals opposed to one. Armed figures. Inscription: 'Here lies Colum, Son of Ruari MacLeod'. Colum (Malcolm) MacLeod, a chief of the MacLeods of Lewis, died between 1515-1524.

(150) (SO)   Inscription: 'Here lies the body of Angus, son of Lord Angus MacDonald of Islay', a grandson of John II, Lord of the Isles. Below, galley with furled sail and banners. Just before 1500.

(172) (N)   The plant scroll of the central panel terminates at the top in an animal's head, above which is a faint pair of shears on the broad inner border. *c.* 1500.

(132) (RO)   Two opposed animals at top of central panel.

(127) (RO)   Vertically to the left of the cross is a boat with figures. A sword is to the right.

(144) (N)   At bottom, a casket and shears. Near top, possibly a book.

(175) (RO)   The central plant scroll of eight circles terminates at the foot in an animal. *c.* 1500.

(154)   Foliated cross, galley with furled sail, illegible inscription, plant scrolls springing from the tails of two animals.

(149) (RO)   Figure on horseback followed by dog. Harpist in a boat(?); below, two pairs of opposed animals. Faded inscription at top: 'Here lies Nicolaus'.

(191) (RO)   Large sword. At lower left is an animal biting its own tail. At foot a lid of a casket.

(128) (N)   Long shafted cross with interlaced head. In the top left corner is a spray of foliage and to the right a leonine creature.

(123) (RO)   Viking-type sword hilt at top flanked by an animal and bird – fourteenth century.

(148) (RO)   Two pairs of animals from whose tails spring intertwined plant-scrolls.

(156)   Galley with decorated sternpost, and stag hunt.

GHOSTLY ENCOUNTERS IN THE ABBEY

One bright sunny afternoon Tommy Frankland encountered an invisible force halfway up a set of stairs in the Abbey. It barred his way so effectively he had to retreat. A while later he tried again and there was no impediment. The incident is recounted in Peter Underwood's *Gazetteer of Scottish Ghosts*. In 1973 a young student had a strange experience while on a field study week. She was in the top bunk of one of the two-bunk bedrooms the Iona Community has on the first floor of the cloister buildings. She turned onto her side so she was facing the wall, then felt both cold and unusually anxious, so she turned onto her left side to come face to face with some kind of human-faced entity. After gazing at it in fear for some time she pulled back against the wall – which was very cold – and yelled for her friend Edith, asleep in the bottom bunk. Edith leapt out of the bed and slammed right into the now open door before switching on the light. After they calmed down the two women played cards for the rest of the night. Later investigation proved the door could never be opened as far as it was that night because of a bump in the linoleum, and no one could walk silently in the squeaky corridor outside. The morning after the incident the two students met a third woman who had seen something moving across her room before gradually disappearing, 'as the light seemed to grow much brighter before dwindling back to normal'. It had happened twenty minutes before the first two young women had calmed down enough to note the time. That night the trio resolved to sit up in the Common Room rather than sleep in their bedrooms. The lecturer who tried to chase them off to bed eventually got the story out of them. To their amazement the lecturer, an ordained minister, laughed – she had seen 'him' many times before and knew he meant no harm. Despite this the three teenagers decided to sleep in shifts for the next few nights. Eighteen years after the incident the witness reported it to paranormal researcher Tom Perrott, who published it in the *Ghost Trackers Newsletter* of Chicago in June 1991.

THE LOST LIBRARY

The room over the chapter house is traditionally identified as the monastic library. Legends of the lost library of Iona have been circulating for centuries, but they can be traced to Hector Boece, who claimed he had based his *History of the Scottish People* on a mysterious book which he found on Iona and that no one else ever saw. The accuracy of Boece's work can be judged by his claim that the Scots King Fergus II, assisting Alaric the Goth in the sacking of Rome, brought away a chest of books as plunder, which he presented to the monastery at Iona. The Sack of Rome was in 412, over 150 years before Columba landed on Iona. So, no lost books from the great libraries of Rome then. However, the Columban monastery had a scriptorium and must have produced many illustrated manuscripts. Some, such as the *Book of Kells*, have survived, but what happened to the other books? The usual suspects are destruction during the Viking raids, or theft and dispersal at the Reformation. Or possibly they were hidden for safekeeping. A persistent tradition that the library was taken to Carnburg, one of the Treshnish Islands, and buried there at the Reformation, led St Andrews University archaeology students to dig there in the 1950s, but nothing was found.

ST MARY'S CHAPEL AND TOBAR A'CHEATHAIN

Tobar a'Cheathain, the Well of Ceathan or Kian, a former healing well, is covered by a concrete slab 25m southeast of the Abbey Church. Old people often requested a drink from it on their deathbed. The fragmentary ruin to the southeast over the fence is St Mary's Chapel, probably a chapel for medieval pilgrims which was later used as a burial place for men. One of the medieval roads leads to it.

THE ABBEY MUSEUM***

The museum has the best collection of West Highland carving in Scotland, bringing together well over a hundred Early Christian and medieval stones. Instead of describing each and every stone this section will concentrate on those which have carvings or associations of particular interest. The numbers in brackets are the RCAHMS numbers, as used for grave slabs in the Nunnery, St Oran's Chapel, Cloisters and Nave, and listed in *Argyll 4*. The second number refers to the museum's own system, and you will sometimes find tags with these numbers. The letters refer to the stone's former home when known - 'RO' (Reilig Odhráin), 'N' (Nunnery) and 'SO' (St Oran's Chapel).

(214) 93 (SO)   MacKinnon's Cross. The most striking carving on this shaft of a free-standing cross is the superb griffin from whose tails springs a plant-scroll. The creature may be modelled on one on a capital of the south choir-arcade in the Abbey Church. On the other side

Griffin, MacKinnon's Cross, Abbey
Museum.

the inscription reads, 'This is the cross of Lachlan MacKinnon
and of his son John, Abbot of Iona, made in the year of Our Lord
1489'. John is the same Abbot whose effigy is in the Chancel and
who is associated with MacKinnon's Cave on Staffa. His father
was chief of his clan. A banner near the prow of the galley has a
faint cross on a stepped plinth. The edges of the shaft have paterae
(decorative oval or circular ornamentation) and other devices
including a tiny cat's head. The base, (227) 93, was designed for a
different cross. It has an incised dial with twenty-four rays, three
marked by crosses. Similar dials are also found on cross bases in
Mull, Kilberry and Oronsay. Part of the perimeter of the dial was
trimmed off in the early seventeenth century when the slab was
reused as the upper stone of a pedestal in the church (the pedestal
was dismantled in 1906). The graffiti on the edges are inverted
because the stone was upright in the pedestal.

The most impressive of the monuments in the museum are the five large effigies
of men in armour. Starting from the left:

(207) 108 (SO)   Gilbride MacKinnon's Stone. This powerfully martial effigy
                  marked the resting place of five successive generations of
                  MacKinnons. The worn inscription on the pillow would have
                  read 'Here lies Gilbride MacKinnon with his sons Ewan and

An angel hovers over Gilbride
MacKinnon's shoulder. Abbey Museum.

Cornebellus'. Another inscription on the top edge reads 'Here
lies Finguin son of Cormac and Finlay son of Finguin and
Ewan'. The style of the armour is too late for Gilbride (who
lived around the late thirteenth century) and the monument
was probably erected by his great-grandson, Abbot Finguin, in
the late 1300s. The slab is full of fascinating detail. On the shield,
below the galley, is a beast (a lion?) and otter pursuing a salmon.
This latter image is a wealth-motif taken from the story of the
Norse hero Sigurd in the *Volsung Saga*. Otr was killed by the
Aesir, the Norse gods, when they saw him on the riverbank
with a catch of fish and mistook him for an otter. Otr's family demanded compensation from the Aesir, who as recompense
stuffed Otr's body with dwarf gold and also covered his skin
with gold. Eventually Fafnir commits patricide to get the Otter's
Gold and turns himself into the dragon that Sigurd later slays.
The baseslab is rich with small carved details. At the lower right
a hound pursues a deer. At lower left is a lion. At centre right
a serpentine dragon snakes through foliage. At top right a dog
looks back at its tail. At the top left are two confronted monsters,
possibly a griffon and a manticore.

(210)   An unidentified chief buckling on a mighty sword.

(209) 100 (RO)   An unidentified chief with a long beard, spear in right hand and

sword in belt. On the shield is a winged dragon or wyvern, a battlemented tower and an ornamental border. There was once an animal crest on the helmet but this has faded away. A crouching greyhound lies beneath his feet. Fourteenth – fifteenth century.

(211) 101 (RO)   Lachlan's Stone, fourteenth – fifteenth century. A partly-legible inscription on the pillow, continuing down the left-hand margin of the slab, and giving the names of both the deceased and the sculptor, reads '+ …Lachlan…of Lachlan…and Maelsechlainn O Cuin, mason, fashioned it'. He is buckling on a sword and his feet rest on a dog. There is an angel on each side of the head, the one on the right holding a sword. To the left of the legs is a faint griffin with a claw raised. Both this effigy and 209 have – without any real justification – been identified as the grave slab of Eoghan a' chin bhig (Ewan of the Little Head), the headless ghost who appears on a black horse accompanied by the clashing of chains, whenever any member of the Lochbuy family dies. He was last seen at Maclean's Cross.

(208)   An unidentified chief. Formerly in the Abbey Church, where it was vandalised in the mid-nineteenth century. His beard is plaited and he is armed with a spear and sword. On the shield is a galley and a lion, while the other shoulder strap carries a whelk shell, possibly for use as a horn.

Other stones of interest include:

(204) 105   Grave slab formerly in the chancel of the Nunnery Church, where it was broken by the collapse of the vault in 1830 when Rae Wilson excavated there. In 1772 the stone was covered in cow dung but Pennant bribed the locals to uncover it. The last prioress Anna Maclean died in 1543. Angels support the pillow for her head; above is a mirror and comb between turrets. At her waist, nestling into her cloak, are two lapdogs, one with a bell at its neck and the other with a ball. In the Middle Ages nuns were addicted to pets of all kind, especially small dogs, and for centuries bishops tried in vain to prevent this. No doubt Prioress Anna doted on these dogs. Under her feet is 'Sancta Maria ora pro me'. This prayer was addressed to the Virgin Mary, whose effigy was on the other panel, now broken off, which had a crowned Mary on a throne with the Child in her arms and the sun and moon. The Nunnery was dedicated to the Virgin.

(80) (SO)   St Oran's Cross. This is the earliest High Cross, erected in 750-800 and now in fragments. The top arm includes four roundels

with serpents whose jaws enclose small bosses. Below are two beasts back-to-back and third one tucked under to the left. At the top of the shaft are the Virgin (with halo) and Child between two angels. To the left is Daniel(?) with a lion, and there are four beasts to the right. On the back (not currently visible) is a harpist (probably David), and to the right an enthroned figure (Pilate?) facing a man (Christ?) while the serpents on the top arm menace a head(?).

(60) 'St Columba's Pillow', in the iron cage in which it was displayed in the Abbey. This water-worn boulder with a ringed cross was found about 1870 between Cladh an Diseirt and Clachanach. The name is derived from Adomnan, who writes that Columba had 'for a pillow a stone, which stands to this day as a kind of monument beside his grave'. The style of the cross, however, dates it to the eighth century at the earliest. The 'Pillow' is another example of the over-enthusiastic desire to match recovered artefacts and structures to ancient textual sources, the kind of problem that has long plagued archaeologists in the biblical lands. The story of the pillow has also inspired later cross-decorated rounded beach boulders, a type of monument almost unique to Iona: there are five in the museum.

(69) Kali's Stone for Fugl. Found in 1962 close to Reilig Odhráin. One half of a late tenth or eleventh century rectangular slab whose greatest item of interest is the inscription in Norse runes: 'Kali, son of Olvir, laid this stone over Fugl his brother'. It has an initial saltire cross, and smaller crosses separate the individual words.

(95) 22 Fragment of the shaft of a Scandinavian cross crudely carved from dark stone. One face has debased interlace with, below to the left, a dragon whose tail is knotted round its body. On the other face is a now hard-to-see but extraordinary carving of a ship containing several men, some of whom appear to be holding spears and swords, and possibly hauling on oars. Above them on the left there is a larger figure of a smith with a hammer. In front of him are a punch, pincers and shears. Above his head is another smith's tool (bellows?). At the centre a pole carries a head(?). To the right of the ship is an otter, and further up the shaft is a curving contoured band, perhaps belonging to a ribbon-beast. At the top of one edge is a small serpentine creature resembling a dolphin. The prominence of the smith in the imagery suggests a link to either Weyland, the Norse smith-god, or Regin, the treacherous smith who forges the sword Gram with which Sigurd kills the dragon Fafnir, but the carving is too imprecise for any positive identification.

The clach-bràth, the Day of Judgement Stone, bottom left. The broken basin is hidden behind the triple cross-incised stone. Abbey Museum.

(99) (RO)   The Day of Judgement Stone. This is not easy to identify as part of it is currently obscured behinds a larger monument bearing three inscribed crosses. It is the composite lid of an Early Christian cross-base formed of two slabs with cramp-holes showing where they were joined and a shared central socket 0.62m by 0.3m. One slab was trimmed for reuse as a grave slab and bears a faint ringed cross and the other pierced with a second smaller socket, presumably to support a smaller cross. The main point of interest, however, is the broken, basin-shaped hollow (currently hidden). This was the famous clach-bràth, the Day of Judgement Stone. For centuries it lay near the edge of the path to St Oran's Chapel and visitors were invited to rotate small stones in the hollow, three times sunwise, *deisul*, 'thus Druidically performing the rites of sun worship on the way to the worship of God' (Neil M. Gunn, *Off In A Boat*). Occasionally this was reported as being for personal divination or for luck, but most of the descriptions are unequivocal: once the basin was worn through, the Day of Judgement would come. (You have to wonder about the world-view of people who wished to speed up the Apocalypse.) The tradition is recorded by Sacheverell, Pennant and all later visitors. Sacheverell describes the small

stones as 'three noble globes of white marble' which the Synod of Argyll ordered to be thrown into the sea, 'perhaps hoping that when these dangerous instruments of it [the end of the world] were removed, it might never come to pass'. Three ordinary stones were substituted and the practice continued until the nineteenth century. It all may have arisen from the confusion between the Gaelic words *bràth* (the day of judgement) and *bra* or *clach-bràthann* (a quernstone). Although, of course, the re-used crossbase looks nothing like a quernstone. And, curiously, Sacheverell describes the marble stones as being 'placed on *three* stone basons' (my emphasis). Could there have been an earlier quernstone or quernstone-like Day of Judgement Stone which was later replaced by the recycled crossbase? I have no idea, but Sacheverell's description, and its variance from all later reports, is intriguing. You will note, however, that the destroyed state of the Day of Judgement Stone (or stones) means that the end of the world should have turned up some time ago.

(130) 65 (RO)   Grave slab. The narrow central panel contains two intertwined stems which terminate at one end in a dragon's head.

(147) 78 (RO)   Grave slab of a priest. On the right, a chalice and book, on the left, a pair of animals linked by their tails to intertwined plant scrolls. The carvings are very faint.

(146) 79 (RO)   Grave slab of a smith. At the foot, two small anvils and possibly a third larger one. Other grave slabs have opposed beasts, a chalice, a bell and a narrow double spiral ending in a single dragon's head.

(84)   St Matthew's Cross. Before this badly-damaged High Cross was removed to the Museum in 1994 it stood in the still-extant base 12m west of the Abbey Church. On the lower shaft you can just about make out the temptation of Adam and Eve with the serpent coiled round the tree.

6

THE NORTH OF THE ISLAND

This chapter starts immediately north of the Abbey and proceeds around the north of the island in an anti-clockwise direction. In the field north of the Abbey is a small rocky outcrop which in the Ritchies' 1928 map is called Cnoc nam marbh, the Mound of the Dead. A small standing stone has been erected at the edge of the private courtyard behind the Iona Community shop. The shop foyer is almost always open and provides toilets and an escape from the weather. To the north of the Iona Gallery and Pottery (NM 286246) once stood Na Crossan Mòr, 'The Great Crosses', both removed long before 1876.

CLADH AN DISEIRT*

NM 289248. This fragmentary ruin, in the second field north of the Abbey, is all that remains of the burial ground and associated chapel of the hermitage ('cladh' here translates as stones and 'diseirt' means desert, which, drawing on the experience of the early Christian hermits in the deserts of Egypt and the Holy Land, can mean hermitage). Hermits are recorded at Iona in 1164; they were both part of the monastic community and apart from it. The hermitage may have had a living room next to a simple oratory. A hermit was often buried in or beside his cell. As late as 1866 the two currently upright stones supported a trilithon-like lintel, leading both Pococke and Pennant to name the monument a cromlech, although there is nothing prehistoric here. An old name for the site is Cladh Iain, 'John's graveyard', which implies the chapel may have been dedicated to St John.

'ST COLUMBA'S TABLE' *

Adomnan describes a flat stone of division on which the monks' grain was placed for luck before it was ground, and tradition points to this 'St Columba's Table' being a 'Chlach mhor', 'the big boulder', an Ice Age granite relic in the same field as Cladh an Diseirt, nearer the road. It is too far from the monastery to be part of the refectory which was supposedly centred on it. James Drummond, in *Sculptured Monuments in Iona and The West Highlands* (1881) notes that it is some-

Cnoc nam marbh, the Mound of the Dead. I can find no tradition connected to the
name. Behind is the ruined sixteenth-century Bishop's House.

Cladh an Diseirt, showing its relationship with the Abbey.

times said that Columba was buried under the rock. In this field was found the stone erroneously called 'St Columba's Pillow' (see Abbey Museum).

IOMAIR TOCHAIR, 'RIDGE OF THE CAUSEWAY'*

NM 285247. This flat-topped straight grassy embankment, to the north of the MacLeod Centre, runs along the southwest side of what was Lochan Mor, the big lochan, drained in 1750 for peat. It has been the source of much speculation – it was meant to have been built to provide access to the Hermit's Cell, or it was a constitutional walk for bishops – but is probably just a raised causeway across boggy ground. There were once trees on each side.

CLACHANACH

NM 286247. Adjoining the dwelling on the west side of the road north of Iomair Tochair is the site of the now-vanished burial site Cill (or Cladh) mo Neachdain, dedicated to the seventh century St Nechtan. Reeves (1857) combines references to Cill mo Neachdain and another lost burial ground, Cill mo Ghobhannain, and equates them both with Martin's 1695 reference to 'a piece of ground between the church and the gardens, in which murderers and children that died before baptism were buried'. Ghobhannain (aka Ghobannain, Gobnenn) was a Celtic smith-god. The Ritchies (*Iona Past and Present*) mention an old saying associated with the site:

Right: The Duchess's Cross with Iomair na h-Achd immediately behind.

Opposite: 'Columba's Table'. At 1.8m high it is perhaps too tall for a monkish table even in those heroic times.

'I buried my nine daughters as seven in Cill mo Neachdain in Iona'. The meaning is that there were two double burials and one triple burial. In the first decade of the twentieth century an earthwork to the north was levelled to build an extension to the rear of the house. Two metres down were the carefully-buried bones of a small horse. This attracted huge attention, as Adomnan describes Columba on his last day saying goodbye to a much-loved white workhorse, which wept for the saint's impending death (the scene is represented in a famous 1923 painting by John Duncan, *St Columba Bidding Farewell to the White Horse*). Except for some teeth, the remains disintegrated. A harvest folklore survival was also recorded at Clachanach. E Mairi MacArthur in *Iona: The Living Memory of a Crofting Community* describes how when the time came for spring ploughing the deireidh bhuain, the 'last sheaf' from the previous autumn's harvest, was ceremonially taken down from the kitchen wall and fed to the horse. 'At Clachanach it was usually a single narrow sheaf, about 1 to 1 and a half inches in diameter and decorated with ribbon. It was never forgotten'. Similar harvest customs – including sheafs called A'Mhaighdean, 'the maiden', and A'Chailleach, 'the old woman' – were widespread throughout Iona and Scotland; the practice mostly died out in the 1950s but at least one house on Mull still had a deireidh bhuain in 1989. Across the road is the pleasantly lichened Duchess's Cross, erected to the Duchess of Argyll in 1878. Immediately to the north is Iomair na h-Achd, 'The Ridge of The Acts or Statutes', now barely noticeable as a slight ridge parallel to the road. In 1609 Andrew Knox, Bishop of the Isles, summoned nine West Highland Chiefs to Iona, possibly to this ridge, and

Tràigh Bhàn Nam Manach, the White Strand of the Monks, home of Iona's favourite ghostly Vikings. Eilean Annraidh is in the background.

made them swear to uphold the Statutes of Iona, measures designed to reduce the internecine clan warfare, ensure the support of the Reformed Church, and start integrating the Hebrides into Lowland Scottish culture. Iona was chosen because it was neutral territory – no clan had its base there – and because an oath sworn on holy ground was binding. Further north on the west side of the road is the remains of an àtha or corn-drying kiln, which from a distance does resemble a prehistoric cairn, so it easy to see how earlier writers confused them.

TRÀIGH BHÀN NAM MANACH, 'WHITE STRAND OF THE MONKS'*

This lovely stretch of sand was the scene of the third consecutive slaughter of Iona monks by Vikings, when the Abbot and fifteen brethren were martyred in 986. The dark, steep rock at the north end of the beach is said to be stained with the blood of the victims. The rock is called Sgeir nam Màrt, 'Rock of the Cows' – it was used for landing cattle before the pier in the village was built. Peter Underwood in *Gazetteer of Scottish Ghosts* reports a story told to him by his friend Tommy Frankland, once a member of the Iona Community. Another member, John MacMillan, was walking one midsummer evening to the north of the island, and decided to call on Mrs Ferguson, an elderly, blind lady he had befriended. But although he had visited her

The ringing rock, Port na Fraing.

many times, he could not find her croft. And then he could not find the croft of
his friend John Campbell either. All familiar landmarks and buildings had vanished.
By now it was bright moonlight. As he reached the White Sands, he saw fourteen
Viking longboats being rowed from behind Eilean Annraidh, the islet immediately
to the north, and fierce warriors shouting as they reached the beach where a group
of monks were gathered. To his horror the invaders proceeded to kill all the monks.
The Vikings left his sight for a time he could not measure – an hour or a minute, he
could not say – then returned with cattle and booty, while the sky turned red from
the burning Abbey. The plunder was loaded, and the longboats pushed off into the
night. The entire episode had been completely silent. That night, MacMillan, an
artist, sketched the emblems he had seen on the longboat sails. The British Museum
confirmed them as being tenth century. Underwood reports that on another occasion the Edinburgh artist, F.C.B. Cadell, along with three companions, also saw the
ghostly invasion, and their reaction was that they were watching a rehearsal for a
historical pageant or movie. A different account says Cadell saw the ghosts at the
Hermit's Cell. John Harries, in *The Ghost Hunter's Road Book,* adds more supernatural details: ghostly chanting in the Abbey as the invaders draw near – sometimes
in daylight – and one sighting taking place while an air raid alert was underway in
Glasgow in autumn 1941, causing some concern in the operations room of RAF
Fighter Command at Raigmore, Inverness, which wondered if it might be enemy
activity. These ghostly Vikings are Iona's most commonly reported phantoms.

The Well of Age on the summit of Dùn-I.

In the grass west of the beach is Tobar magh luinge or lunga, either 'Well of the Plain of the Ship' (a Columban monastery was founded at Magh Lunge in Tiree) or a dedication to the seventh century St Moluag. There is nothing to see now. At the southern end of the sands, and north of the only house on the coast, is a tiny creek called Port na Fraing, 'bay of the Frenchman'. Locate the huge erratic of pink granite balanced near the shore and move just to the north: here is a smaller rock with a hollow in the top. This is a ringing rock – hitting it with a pebble traditionally left in the hollow produces several distinct notes. The hollow itself may be man-made.

Just south of Cnoc Buidhe, south of Lagandorain, is the intriguingly named Cnoc na carcuil (or carcair), 'Hill of the [hermit's] cell' or 'Hill of the prison', and north of Lagandorain is Cnoc an t–Suidhe, 'Hill of the Seat', on which tradition sites Columba's meditation spot. Alison Johnston of the St Columba Hotel is quoted in Marc Alexander's *Enchanted Britain* regarding the next beach around the northern tip of the island, Traigh an t–Suidhe ('Beach of the Seat'): 'One night a couple of girls were camping there and began experimenting with an ouija board. It certainly triggered off something because minutes later they were hammering at the door of the Iona Community. Next morning they were put on the first ferry to Fionnphort'.

DÙN-I AND THE FOUNTAIN OF YOUTH**

NM 283252. Dùn-I is the highest point on the island. A marked footpath leaves from the road north of Clachanach. There is an old belief that good luck follows those who have made the ascent seven times. The much-reduced cairn at the top was erected in 1897 to commemorate the 1300th anniversary of the death of Columba. Fifty-five metres due north of the cairn is a small triangular pool, Tobar na h-Aois, variously translated as the Well of Age or of Beauty, the Fountain of Youth or the Pool of Healing. The Scottish mystic Fiona Macleod (William Sharp) regarded the well as a vision site. In *Iona* he wrote that he climbed Dùn-I because, 'if anywhere, I thought that from there I might see the Divine Forges, or at least might discover a hidden way, because of the power of that water, touched on the eyelids at sunlift, at sunset, or at the rising of the moon....I wetted my eyelids, as I had so often done before (and not always vainly, though whether vision came from the water, or from a more quenchless spring within, I know not)'. Up until the 1920s the tradition was that bathing the face in the water at sunset would roll back the years – although whether the transformation was physical or spiritual is unclear. Certainly this author's recourses to the dark waters have had not the slightest impact on the ravages of time. Macleod also eulogised the spiritual seekers who made the pilgrimage to the well: 'Solitary, these: not only because the pilgrim…must fare hither alone, and at dawn, so as to touch the healing water the moment the first sunray quickens it--but solitary, also, because those who go in quest of this Fount of Youth are the dreamers and the Children of Dreams, and these are not many, and few come to this lonely place'.

One of the strangest legends associated with Iona is that of St Bride of the Isles, Muime Chriosd, 'the Foster-Mother of Christ'. The story in its folkloric form is confused and contradictory because of the overlap between three female characters called Bride/Bridget. The original Bride was the beautiful young Celtic goddess of Spring. In the seventh century there was an Irish saint, St Bride of Kildare, who became very popular in Scotland. Much of her life is legendary, although she does appear to have actually existed. Linking these two, and acting as a bridge between paganism and Christianity ('the pagan goddess in a threadbare Christian cloak' – Sir James Frazer, *The Golden Bough*), is the categorically fictional figure of St Bride of the Isles.

Fiona Macleod in *The Washer of the Ford* synthesized the various Bride legends circulating in the Hebrides into a coherent narrative with rich, poetic language; he makes Dùn-I the centre of this Bride's story. Dùghall Donn, the son of King Hugh of Ireland, was exiled for supposedly impregnating a noblewomen called Morna, although he swore he was innocent. With him into exile he took his infant daughter Bride, the product of the supposed liaison, the mother having died in childbirth. Aodh, a Druid at the Irish court, claimed that Dùghall was indeed innocent: Bride was the result of a virgin birth, and she had a great destiny.

Dùghall and Bride were shipwrecked on Iona, where the tiny baby prayed in a language unknown to her father and then prophesied about her own future in Irish. The pair were taken under the wing of the Druids, who also recognized Bride's status, having their own prophecy of a maiden, product of a virgin birth, whose breasts would give milk to the Prince of the World. Dùghall was required to change his name to Dùvach, and he lived the life of a poor herdsman on the southeast slope of Dùn-I, his royal identity known only to Cathal the Arch-Druid. When Bride was nine years old she entered a trance state and repeated the prayer she had spoken as a baby, but otherwise she grew up a normal young woman, although an exceptionally serene, tender-hearted and beautiful young woman who was adored by animals and birds and all nature – very much the Goddess of Spring incarnate. Dùvach married and had seven sons, and one day the eldest, Conn, reproached Bride for not having taken a husband: 'Idle are these pure eyes, O Bride, not to be as lamps at thy marriage-bed'. 'Truly, it is not by the eyes that we live,' she replied, and passed her hands before her eyes; when she took them away the sockets were empty. After awe-struck apologies were made, another pass of the hands revealed eyes where they should have been.

One beautiful spring morning, the very day specified in the Druidic prophecy, Bride climbed Dùn-I, where in a state of religious ecstasy she watched three Druids ritually greet the sun. At the Well of Age she rescued a young lamb from a falcon; the lamb nestled in her arms while the raptor meekly sat on her shoulder. Taking a drink from the pool she was startled by a reflection in the water of a beautiful, divine woman. The branches of two rowan trees merged to form a green arch, with a crown at the top. The rowan-berries – ripe months before their time – dripped deep red drops from this crown, as if of blood. A white blackbird sang a bittersweet, rapturous song from the centre of the meshed rowans. A white dove guided Bride forward into the numinous gateway, and she followed 'with a dream-smile upon her face and her eyes full of the sheen of wonder and mystery, as shadowy waters flooded with moonshine'. Upon entering the holy vortex, Bride was taken by angels to Bethlehem on the eve of the Nativity. She assisted Mary with the birth of her child, wrapped him in her humble plaid, so becoming Brigdhe-nam-Brat, 'Bride of the Mantle', and stayed with the Holy Family to breast-feed the infant Jesus. After a year and a day she was returned to Iona by angels. A painting by John Duncan in the National Gallery of Scotland (*St Bride*, Code G510A2) shows the divine journey – two beautiful winged angels, their gorgeous robes decorated with scenes of the life of Christ, gently support the praying Bride. She is dressed in white, her long hair flowing freely, and her eyes are closed in religious rapture. Seabirds follow them and a seal skims the waves below.

Illegal whisky distilling was carried out at both Glac Domhain, a deep gully on the west of Dùn-I, and Am Briuthas Beag, just south of Traigh Mor; and the marshy Lòn na poit-Dhubh, south-west of Dùn-I, is where the poit-Dhubh, 'black pot' (still) was hidden from the customs men.

Which is the mystical site and which the agricultural structure? First: the Hermit's Cell.

Second: Sloc nam Ball.

Third: Sloc Srath Mugain.

THE HERMIT'S CELL**

NM 276249. This small ruin has been the source of speculation and spiritual wish-fulfillment – as well as mystical experiences – since at least the eighteenth century. Much of this has focused on the name. The 1878 first edition of the Ordnance Survey gives it as Tigh nan Cuildich, 'House of the Culdees', another version being Cabhan Culdish, 'Culdee's Cell', but both of these were pseudo-learned translations, inspired by the then vogue for the Culdees. These monks were an austere reform movement who became the focus of a persistent Victorian spiritual-historical enthusiasm, in which the ascetic, intellectual Culdees came to be seen as a cipher of both the antiquarians' beloved Druids and a bulwark against decadent Popish Catholicism; more extreme views claimed Columba or some of his companions as Culdees, even though they lived long before the movement's origins in eighth-century Ireland. Culdees are recorded on Iona in 1164, prob-ably as a small community living alongside but separate from the main monastery – Culdees and monastic brothers lived in mutual regard in numerous monasteries in Scotland and Ireland. The actual name, Cobhan Cuildich, means 'the remote hollow', but the Culdean association has survived and today the site is universally known as the Hermit's Cell. The site is not at first appearance very pre-possess-ing. The wall footings are low and oval with an entrance to the south. The *Old Statistical Account* of 1795 describes a path from this entrance, 'to a small hillock, with the remains of a wall on each side of the walk which grows wider to the hillock. There are evident traces of the walls of the walk taking a circuit round and enclosing the hillock'. The path and walls are no longer visible. About 30m to the north is a large enclosure built around a massive rock outcrop, with irregular walls of large boulders. Inside there is a well (look for the circle of stones around the reeds) and the remains of a rectangular structure by one of the walls. Skene (*Celtic Scotland*) makes the suggestion that the Hermit's Cell may have been the 'more remote place in the wilds' to which St Columba withdrew for prayer, perhaps even where Adomnan describes Columba fighting all day in a wild part of Iona against black demons intent on impaling him and his monks with iron spikes. Columba fought them to a standstill by taking on the armour of the apostle Paul, but the demons were only defeated by the arrival of reinforcements in the form of a troupe of angels. Although the hut may have been rebuilt at least once, archaeologists cautiously admit it may originally be a beehive hut from the Dark Ages. More prosaic interpretations see it as a post-medieval structure for animals, and the large enclosure to the north is almost certainly a sheep or cattle fank dating from no earlier than the nineteenth century. However, in the absence of excavation nothing can be said for certain about the date. MacArthur (1995) has an illuminating incident in which an old Iona woman, keen to see this 'Hermit's Cell' that so many visitors made such a fuss about, declared that it was just a circle for milking cows in, as she had done in the 1890s. And indeed there are other such remains scattered around the hills – at, for example, Sloc nam Ball (NM 272253) and Sloc Srath Mugain, both on the coast to the northwest. My contention is that these three structures all have the same agricultural function, but that the Hermit's Cell has received all the attention, and all the spiritual investment, because (a) of the name and the Culdees association (b) it is in a better condition than the other two sites and (c) it is relatively easy to get to.

Mystical associations, however, continue to this day at the Hermit's Cell. Francis Thompson, in *Ghosts Spirits and Spectres of Scotland,* says the artist F.C.B. Cadell was painting on his own near here in 1937 when he saw ghostly Viking warriors whose knees were at the level of the ground (see Tràigh Bhàn Nam Manach). Many visitors (often those with a spiritual outlook) claim to have experienced a sense of the numinous here. Robert Ogilvy Crombie, who reported several encounters with nature spirits at Findhorn, Edinburgh and Rosemarkie in the 1960s, met the god Pan here. The account in Paul Hawken's *The Magic of Findhorn* describes how Crombie was in the centre of the Cell facing east when he saw a large figure laying in the grass, dressed in a monk's brown habit with the hood up. The figure rolled back the hood and rose up to reveal himself as Pan, immense and smiling. He said, 'I am the servant of Almighty God, and I and my subjects are willing to come to the aid of mankind in spite of the way he has treated us and abused nature, if he affirms belief in us and asks for our help'. Crombie saw it as a reconciliation between the Nature Kingdom and man. The account says Pan was 'facing *us*' although we are not told who was there with Crombie. One of the more interesting developments in the growth of the Findhorn Community, the beacon of New Age philosophy in action, is the way Crombie's meetings with elves, fauns and Pan, and other founder members' deep interest in UFOs and alien contact, have both been effectively written out of the Community's history.

One hundred metres north-north-west of the Hermit's Cell is Tobair na Gaoithe Tuath, 'Well of the North Wind', now a rather disappointing puddle between large boulders. Sailors and others brought offerings here to summon up a wind from the north. This was one of four similar magic wells, but the locations of the wells of the south, east and west winds are now lost (see also the stone trough outside the Abbey Church). In *A Trip From Callander to Staffa and Iona,* published in 1894, Malcolm Ferguson claims all four wells were under the control of a family whose forebears arrived with Columba. When required they would go the well of the desired wind and perform 'the usual mystic ceremony', and the wind would change immediately. By the late nineteenth century the family was defunct 'and the charm lost for ever'. Ferguson, who was only on Iona for a short time, obtained this information from a local guide, so it is possible there was some legend-embroidering going on.

DUN MHANANNAIN

This hill is named after Manannan, or Manaun, a widely-worshipped Celtic sea-god. He is a master of trickery, shape-changing, illusion and magic, and often gave magical gifts to the heroes he chose to assist. He also creates storms and wrecks ships. His pigs are killed and eaten one day and alive again the next, and he is often associated with rebirth. Swire (1964) mentions a tradition that a white horse was brought to Manannan here every nine years, which may be a conflation of the St Michael horse-rituals associated with Sithean Mòr. Fiona Macleod in *Iona* relates a legend told to him by a Gaelic farmer named Macarthur. Manannan's body 'was made of a green wave. His hair was of wrack and tangle, glistening with spray; his robe was of windy foam; his feet, of white sand'. In human form, he fell in love with a beautiful woman named Dèarsadh-na-Ghréne ('Sunshine'). He brought her to Iona in September, and she was happy, but when winter set in he saw that she was sickening to death, so he changed her into a seal with the words: 'You shall be a sleeping woman by day, and sleep in my dùn here on Iona: and by night, when the dews fall, you shall be a seal, and hear me calling to you from a wave, and shall come out and meet me'. This is one of many seal-women legends from the coasts and islands of Scotland, although the 'benevolent transformation by sea-god' motif is unusual.

DUN BHUIRG*

NM 265246. There are only scanty remains to be seen of this small Iron Age fort, dating from 100 BC to AD 200. Marsden in *Sea-Road of the Saints* identi-

Uamh Anna Bhig a'Phuinnsean, 'Cave of little Anne of the Poison'. Nothing is known of little Anne, or whether she was victim or poisoner.

fies it as the hill Adomnan called 'great fortress', although most writers see the location as being Dùn-I. From this place Columba saw a rain-cloud which he predicted would bring a plague of ulcers to an area of Ireland, and immediately despatched the monk Silnan armed with blessed bread. Water in which Silnan dipped the bread cured all the afflicted. There is no foundation for the spurious nineteenth-century tradition that Dun Bhuirg was a site of Druidic pilgrimage. Fiona MacLeod had once seen a ghost which he identified as 'the Culdee, Oran', at Cul Bhuirg, a furlong (200m) to the west, and so never went that way again at night. To the southeast, near the dwelling called Culbhuirg (NM 270240) layers of bone mixed with charcoal were found sometime before 1857; either an old burial ground or, more probably, a midden. At the far north end of the Machair is Uamh Anna Bhig a'Phuinnsean, 'Cave of little Anne of the Poison'.

GLEANN AN TEAMPUILL

NM 274241. The name of this valley east of Culbhuirg means 'Glen of the Church', although there is no reliable reference or any archaeology to back this up. At the northeast head of the glen, and just to the west of Cnoc na Meirghe, 'signal rock', was Cladh na Meirghe burial ground (NM 277243), formerly used for the burial of unbaptised children. To the north of the glen is Cnoc Urrais, 'Hill of the Urisk' (or Brownie); urisks are supernatural creatures who haunt lonely glens and hills, but I can find no tradition connected to the name.

7

THE WEST OF THE ISLAND

This chapter covers the road and low-lying area across the waist of the island, and the Machair, the grassy plain on the west coast.

The road from the east coast passes Tighshee ('Fairies' House') and Iona Marble at Waterside where you can buy cross-marked stones as a pilgrimage souvenir. The garden of the house called Caol Ithe, near Maol, on the track leading south from the school to the road, is the site of the burial ground Cladh nan Druineach (NM 284237). The site had attracted attention for many years because of the supposed translation, 'the Druids' graveyard'. To give two examples among many, Douglas's map of 1769 calls it Druids' Burial Place, and John Jamieson, in *A Historical Account of the Ancient Culdees of Iona* (1890), noted that potato-planting here uncovered remains 'which the people immediately concluded to be the bones of Druids'. Daniel Wilson in *Prehistoric Annals of Scotland* (1863) describes the work of the Iona Club's excavations in 1833. Six skulls were extracted and each, labelled as 'skull of a Druid from the Hebrides', was presented to Mr Robert Cox of the Edinburgh Phrenological Society. In the accompanying letter Mr Gregory of the Iona Club wrote, 'It is perfectly certain that this place has never been used as a Christian churchyard, or as a place of internment at all, since the establishment of Christianity here by St Columba'. He added that the skulls were 'selected with care by myself, from a much larger number'. Sadly for Druidic enthusiasts the actual translation of Cladh nan Druineach is the 'Burial Ground of the Craftsmen', and the journal *Crania Britannica* declared Gregory's Druid skulls to be eighth or ninth century. Which may mean, if the name is accurate, that they were from the talented teams of stonemasons who carved the freestanding crosses. In 1863 the skulls were in the Museum of the Phrenological Society. By the 1920s the Ritchies say they were in the custody of anatomist Professor McAlister of the Cambridge Anatomical Museum.

Next to Maol is Bol-leithne, 'Eithne's fold', Eithne being Columba's mother, although the name more probably derives from a later person with the same name. This is also the place Wentworth Huyshe identifies with 'Cuuleilne', mentioned in Adomnan's *Life* as the site of one of the saint's miracles. The monks were returning in the evening, weary from harvest work. At a place midway

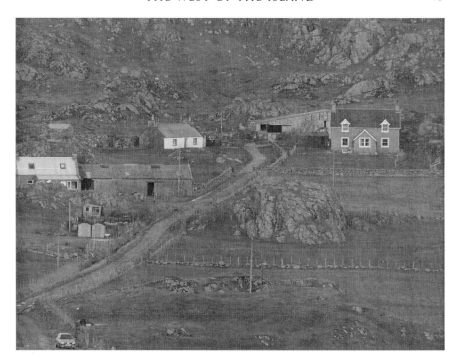

Maol: in this area the monks received telepathic support from Columba.

Sìthean Mòr, with Sìthean Beg, the 'little fairy mound', behind.

Landing pad for angels and home to fairies: Sìthean Mòr at sunset.

between the machair and the monastery, they had a variety of uplifting experiences: enchanting fragrances, a sense of joy that removed sadness and weariness, and 'a certain burning as of fire, not painful, but as it were soothing', and their heavy loads became as nothing. Baithene, the monastery superintendent, one of Columba's original companions from Ireland and his successor as Abbot, told the brethren it was Columba's spirit visiting them, as the saint was concerned because they were tired and late. On the main road, a hillock on the north side, to the west of Cnoc Orain (named for St Oran – see Reilig Odhráin), is Cnoc na h'Anatach, 'Hill of the Breathing'. A young girl searching for a lost sheep in the south of the island stumbled on a man in a cave killing the stolen beast. He gave chase and was about to catch her when the appearance of a group of men caused him to flee the island; the girl collapsed on the Cnoc, told the story, and expired.

SÌTHEAN MÒR/CNOC NAN AINGEAL **

Outside the Abbey complex, this mound is probably the most mystico-spiritual site on the island, and the source of a host of legends, customs and fictions. One of its names, Cnoc nan Aingeal, 'Hill of the Angels', derives from a famous passage in Adomnan's *Life*: Columba said to the brethren, 'To-day I wish to go alone to the western plain of our island; therefore let none of you follow me'. But a 'cunning and prying' Brother went another way, hid on a hillock and saw Columba praying, standing up with arms out on what Adomnan called *Colliculus Angelorum,* the hillock of the angels. Celestial beings in white flew down and spoke to the saint, but then noticed they were under surveillance and flew off. Back at the monastery an angry Columba discovered the identity of the spy, but instead of decreeing a punishment he took the man aside and told him not to reveal what he had seen. It was only after Columba had died that the monk solemnly revealed what he had witnessed that day. The monk had probably hidden on the small outcrop of Cnoc na h'Anatach. Adomnan also describes how, at a much later date than the angelic visitation, a long drought was ended by a procession to the hill with Columba's white tunic and books written in the saint's own hand, which were read aloud on the hill. Adomnan dates this to fourteen years before he wrote the *Life.*

An entirely different tradition comes from the mound's other name, Sìthean Mòr, 'the big fairy mound' (on the other side of the road, close to the fence running north from the end of the road, is the small, rocky Sìthean Beg, 'the small fairy mound'). The most common story associated with Sìthean Mòr (recorded in Campbell's *Superstitions of the Western Highlands* and elsewhere) has two men on the way back from fishing hearing music coming from the mound and joining in the dancing within. One, however, remembered the fairies' aversion to iron and stuck a fishhook in the door while the other went in with his string of fish. Assisted by the iron get-out-of-the-fairy-mound-free device, the first man left when he had enough of the revels, but had to wait twelve months before he could return to free his friend, who was still dancing and holding the fish. Needless to say, as soon as he was released the fish stank to high heaven. In an alternative version, noted in MacArthur (1990), both men were hunchbacks – the one who left early was free of his hunch, but the other was given a second one. Variants of this hunchback tale occur all over Scotland; as here, the first man pleases the fairies by melodiously singing 'Wednesday, Thursday' to complete the fairies' own 'Monday, Tuesday' song, but the second man is punished because he offers 'Friday, Saturday' in a cracked voice. Swire (1964) describes the experience of a doctor friend who used to holiday on the island; visiting a child with a fever, she found the mother bathing it with water containing the tooth of a fairy dog, an apparently attested cure. The doctor thought the item was a seal tooth. Seeing the paw marks of fairy dogs in the sand brought good luck; to step in them, death.

Fiona Macleod, in *Iona,* tells a moral tale of a fisherman called Coll mac Coll who, while daydreaming on the mound, repeated an old Gaelic saying – 'In the Isle of Dreams God shall yet fulfil Himself anew'. A young, dark-eyed blonde man appeared. He had a leaf of sea-poppy in his hair and knew Coll's name. Coll assumed this was a supernatural being called the Green Harper so he made the sign of the cross and muttered some words of an exorcism, but the stranger asserted he was not in danger. 'And because you can see me and speak to me, I will help you to whatsoever you may wish'. Coll laughed bitterly because the

The Bay at the Back of the Ocean.

things he would wish for – the return of his family and his sweetheart from the dead – he knew he could not have. So he wished for glory and power and the Green Harper waved a stick of hazel 'to open a door that is in the air' to grant the wish. At the last moment Coll changed his mind and wished for 'a warm breast-feather from that grey dove of the woods that is winging home to her young'. When he came to, he was alone, with a great weight lifted from his heart. Walking home, he looked back and saw on the knoll a white noble figure upon the knoll – Columba or an angel. As with many of Macleod's writings, it is hard to tell whether this is a story someone told him or whether he embellished it or made the whole thing up.

Pennant learned from Pococke that on St Michael's Eve the islanders brought all their horses to Sìthean Mòr and rode them sunwise round the hill, 'thus unwittingly dedicating their horses to the sun'. The following day, Michaelmas, was the great festival of the year in this part of the world. Carmichael, in his study of Hebridean folklore *Carmina Gadelica,* says of Michaelmas, 'It is a day when pagan cult and Christian doctrine meet and mingle like lights and shadows on their own Highland hills'. Michael, saint and archangel, was Michael the Victorious, Michael of the white steed, conqueror of the dragon, the patron saint of the sea and sailors, of horses and horsemen. On Làthe Bealltuinn, Beltane (May Day) cattle were driven through fires on the mound in an act of purification. An eight-eenth-century description calls it Cnoc-nan-Ainneal, the hill of the fires. Pennant also reported that the mound had on top a circle of stones, with 'a little cairn in the middle evidently druidical'. MacArthur (1990) notes two other (unattributed) descriptions of the site as 'the ruins of a chapel' and 'a grand place of worship to which they went on white horses mounted. They said an angel sent them here'. A book of 1912, *St Columba,* by Victor Branford, has as its frontispiece a line drawing by John Duncan called 'St Columba on the Hill of Angels'. Two art nou-veau angels hover above a kneeling Columba while the Dove of the Holy Spirit extends its blessing onto the saint. Clearly drawing on Pennant's 'cairn', Duncan places a pair of standing stones carved with elaborate Celtic crosses (based on stones now in the Abbey Museum) on the hill. Sìthean Mòr is a natural mound, and modern archaeologists can find no trace of this 'cairn' or 'chapel'; the con-temporary view is that Pennant had confused the site with somewhere else, and that there never was a structure on top of the mound.

CAMUS CÙL AN T-SAIMH, 'THE BAY AT THE BACK OF THE OCEAN'**

This superb sweep of sand in the bay is almost certainly the location of the crane story related in Adomnan's *Life.* Columba told a monk to look after a crane (the old name for a heron) which he predicted in three days would land, exhausted, having flown from Ireland. After three days of care the bird was ready to return. Columba blessed it and gave it a message which when the heron landed at the monastery in Derry was interpreted by angels to the monks there. Walsh and Bradley suggest that this episode symbolises Columba's rejection of the old pagan conception of the crane as a bird of ill-omen. (Herons feature several times in Columban stories – while in Ireland his pet heron blinds a monk spying on him through a keyhole, and in the Old Irish *Life* he transforms the queen, the mother of his enemy Conall, and her attendant into herons.) Down to the end of the eight-eenth century a ceremony took place here on the night before Maundy Thursday, the day before Easter, known as Diardaoin a Bhrochain Mhòir, 'Thursday of the great porridge'. Alexander Carmichael recorded the custom in *Carmina Gadelica,* having talked in 1860 with a middle-aged Iona man whose father, when young, had taken part in the ceremony. A man walked to his waist into the water and poured an offering of oatmeal, chanting

A Dhè ne mara	*O God of the Sea*
Cuir todhar 's an tarruinn	*Put weed in the drawing wave*
Chon tachair an talaimh	*To enrich the ground*
Chon bailcidh dhuinn biaidh	*To shower on us food*

And the people on the shore took up the chant. Kelp had been collected for fertiliser for centuries; the ceremony was designed to encourage the sea to cast up enough seaweed for the second spring ploughing. Note the reference to the God of the Sea. This is probably Mananan (see Dun Mhanannain) although another candidate may be Shony, a sea-god popular throughout the Hebrides; it is entirely possible Mananan and Shony are the same entity. Fiona Macleod in *Iona* records a young girl running in the shallows on the beach singing, 'Shanny, Shanny, Shanny. Catch my feet and tickle my toes! And if you can, Shanny, Shanny, Shanny, I'll go with you where no one knows!' a contrast to the usual characterisation of Shony as a sailor-killer who would make a death-necklace of their teeth. Shony once captured a girl who refused his love; in punishment he tied her to a rock to drown, and to this day her long brown hair may be seen floating in the waves. In the shallows opposite where the path from the road reaches the shore of the Bay at the Back of the Ocean is a rock called Sgeir na caoineig, 'Rock of the weeper or sea-kelpie', a reference to a supernatural water creature. Whether there is any connection with Mananan or Shony I am unable to tell.

South-south-east of Sìthean Mòr, to the east of the fence, is Lochan na croise, 'Lochlet of the cross', although the name is now obsolete. MacArthur (1995) reports a curious story from the 1880s at Cùldamph, at the south edge of the Machair. When Kate Campbell's husband brought her water from the well because she was sick, the water tasted like wine. The next day a neighbour, Alastair Ruanaich, finding her much improved, told her that particular night in February was St Finnan's Eve, when water turns to wine.

8

THE SOUTH OF THE ISLAND

This chapter covers first, the southwest coast of the island, then the popular path from the Machair to Columba's Bay on the south coast, and finally the southeast coast.

This part of the island is entirely uninhabited and has a different feel to the rest of Iona. Peter Underwood, in *Gazetteer of Scottish Ghosts,* mentions how John MacMillan, a member of the Iona Community, rarely walked in the south because he said he could always smell death there, and Lucy Bruce, who had a house on the island, spoke of crowds of elementals in this area. Ivan Macbeth, perhaps the archetypal New Age visitor, described in his online book *Crystal Hunter* (1999) how when planting crystals around this rough wilderness his vision encompassed 'hidden natural Goddess shrines…huge boulder beings, tiny nature spirits and all sorts of characters in between', although I think these are meant to be symbolic rather than literal. 'Philosopher-architect and mystic' Peter Dawkins, in an inter-view for David Tame's book *Real Fairies,* tells of an experience with fairies here. He had just completed one of his regular courses on nature beings at a hotel on Iona, and the elementals told him they wanted a party. So on the Friday Peter and about forty people trekked to the south loaded with picnics, chocolate – and bal-loons tied to their rucksacks. The only problem was, the balloons kept popping. There was much discussion among the group about the mystical significance of it. Then at midday Peter encountered two fairy beings, the guardians of the energy gateway the group had just asked permission to enter. Not knowing the entities were there, a group member asked Peter, 'Why do our balloons keep popping?' to which the fairies replied, 'Oh, we thought balloons *were* for popping!'

NETTA EMILY FORNARIO AND THE 'PSYCHIC MURDER'

IONA MYSTERY: WOMAN VISITOR'S STRANGE DEATH UNCLOTHED ON HILLSIDE

Those were the headlines in *The Scotsman* of 27 November 1929. The dead woman was Netta Emily Fornario, a thirty-two-year-old upper-middle-class woman of unconventional views whose life and death throws a spotlight on the beliefs of a small pocket of pre-War Britons who embraced mysticism, magic and altered states long before the far-out Sixties.

Ms Fornario had arrived in Iona the previous August, with a female companion and enough luggage to suggest an extended, if not indefinite, stay. The pair lodged first with Mrs MacDonald on the shorefront but when her friend went home Netta moved in with the Cameron family at Traighmor, to the south of the village. Her appearance was striking – tall and intense and, as a member of the anti-establishment, anti-industrial, arts and crafts movement, she wore home-spun clothes and tied her dark hair in two heavy plaits. A beatnik *avant la lettre*. Apparently with enough money not to have to bother earning her living, she had devoted herself to spiritual pursuits. Doorstepped by journalists after the death, Mrs Varney, Fornario's housekeeper in Mortlake Road, Kew, was quoted in *The Scotsman* as saying, 'Several times she said she had been to the "far beyond" and had come back to life after spending some time in another world'. During these trances Netta would cure people by telepathy, and she was interested in practicing all forms of spirit communication. Iona was the perfect place for her because she had been on the island in a previous incarnation.

But Iona did not heal what was probably an escalating mental illness. At night she wrote intensively – never drawing her curtains because she could see the faces of her previous 'patients' in the clouds – or went for long walks exploring the 'mystical' sites of the island, probably most of those described in this book. Underwood (1974), rather over-dramatising things, describes how she spent time in 'a bleak and lonely spot which has no real track leading to it where, it is said, the spirits of the dead hold sway'. But she also became more troubled, more anguished. Her clothes became dishevelled and her speech was filled with incoherent references to visions, spiritual communications and the like. Although she was well-liked for her friendliness and charm some of the islanders clearly thought her mad – not as in eccentric, but as in unbalanced. She started to behave as if someone was after her, and mentioned telepathic attacks.

On Sunday 17 November she rose unusually early and announced that a psychic message had told her to leave Iona. Deaf to protests that there were no ferries on a Sunday she decamped to the jetty. When the impossibility of leaving that day finally sank in she resignedly returned to Traighmor, revealed a second communication had told her to stay, and locked herself in her room. That evening she appeared unusually calm. The following morning she was found to have disappeared. The oil lamps she used for writing were still alight, the fireplace was filled with burned papers and pamphlets, and all her jewellery was neatly arranged. The Camerons searched locally but were not that concerned because of Netta's habit of wandering for hours at night. A second, fuller search was conducted that afternoon. The following day, Tuesday, the Mull police and a large band of volunteers were involved. Two farmers and their dog found her in the afternoon. Some of the newspapers placed the body on Sìthean Mòr, but this was journalistic licence, giving in to the temptation to link a mysterious death with a fairy hill. The actual site was much further south, in the wilds about half a mile or so from the southern coast.

At this point we enter the journo-verse, the space where the facts are shaped into (often contradictory) newspaper accounts, and those stories form the foundation of an edifice of claim and counterclaim inevitable where a death occurs with hints of murder and black magic. As it is now impossible to know exactly what happened, we are dependent on these uncertain interpretations. All the papers were agreed that she was naked, was wearing a silver chain and cross around her neck, and had died of exposure on the cold November night. The *Glasgow Bulletin* wrote: 'The body was lying in a sleeping posture on the right side, the head resting on the right hand.… With the exception of a few scratches on the feet, caused by walking over the rough ground, there were no marks on the body'. *The Scotsman* and several other papers described how she was 'lying on a large cross which had been cut out of the turf, apparently with a knife which was lying nearby'. Then the accounts start to diverge, revealing the hunger for elaboration and sensation. The knife was not at a distance but had to be pried from her hand. It was no ordinary tool but a ritual knife. The silver chain and cross had turned black overnight (if the last time she was seen was Sunday evening, when presumably the silver was untarnished, and she was found on the Tuesday, how did anyone know the jewellery had 'turned black overnight'?) She was not entirely naked, but was wearing a black cloak with occult insignia. She had a peaceful look on her face, or a mask of terror. *The Scotsman* mentioned 'mysterious remarks about blue lights having been seen near the body, and of a cloaked man. A number of letters, said to be of a strange character, have been taken possession of by the police, who, it is also stated, have passed them on to the Procurator Fiscal for his consideration'. Threadlines of conspiracy, of murder, of the supernatural, started to spread out, but nothing was ever heard again of the cloaked man or the strange letters.

The case would probably have been forgotten were it not mentioned in a 1930s occult bestseller, *Psychic Self-Defence*. The author, Dion Fortune (real name Violet Evans), a well-known occultist, had been friends with Netta Fornario – who she knew as 'Mac' – until they had drifted apart because Fortune was uneasy about Netta's ill-advised psychic diving into deep waters inhabited by something called the 'Green Ray elemental contacts'. In *Psychic Self-Defence* Fortune wondered whether Netta had stayed on the astral plane too long, or slipped into an elemental kingdom, but her best bet was that she had been a victim of psychic attack. In a later article Fortune named the assailant – Mina Mathers, widow of MacGregor Mathers, one of the founding members of the ritual magical group the Hermetic Order of the Golden Dawn. After the death of her husband in 1918, Mina had established an offshoot temple called Alpha et Omega. Of which

The gravestone of Netta Fornario, to the north of St Oran's Chapel, Reilig Odhráin.

Netta Fornario was a member. Initially, the idea was semi-plausible. The members of the notoriously fissiparous magical groups were always in dispute and unleashing various supernatural attacks on each other. Their entire lives seemed to be spent in a tragi-comic round of seeking elevated spiritual states, acquiring highfaluting titles, and wallowing in base hatreds. But if Mina Mathers had hexed Netta to death it was a doubly impressive feat, as by November 1929 the ogress had already been dead for sixteen months.

The case was looked at again by Francis King in his influential *Ritual Magic in England* (1972). King believed that Netta was under psychic attack – or at least she believed she was – although he concedes most people will come down on the side of mental illness. He offers a possible explanation for the blackened jewellery – vegetarians who ate eggs had such high sulphur compounds in their sweat that they could turn silver black in thirty minutes. He notes Netta's interest in an ancient village to the south (Laraichean) but that she had not been there because of difficulty of access – as she was found within half a mile of it, she may have been on her way there. King also says the black cloak Netta was (allegedly) wearing was that of the Hiereus, an important officer in the Golden Dawn.

For his book *Scotland's Unsolved Mysteries of the Twentieth Century* (from which I have taken many of the details here), Richard Wilson tracked down Calum

Cameron, who was twelve in 1929 when Netta stayed with his parents at Traighmor. According to Calum, the knife was just an ordinary kitchen knife, and there was no cross carved in the turf – Netta was just digging in the ground, maybe to get to the fairies inside.

Netta Emily Fornario was interred in Reilig Odhráin on the Friday after her death. Most of the islanders attended the funeral. An aunt and uncle were contacted in London but could not make it so a solicitor made the arrangements. Netta was estranged from her father, an Italian doctor. On 5 December 1929 *The Scotsman* reported that he had been seized with a terrible feeling of anxiety regarding his daughter. Two days later a telegram arrived announcing that her body had just been discovered.

The incident has inspired a poem by Helen Cruickshank (1886-1975), 'Ballad of Lost Ladye', in which the knife was to be used to open the fairy hill and 'let oot the queen'. At the end the shepherd finds her dead, with a beatific expression on her face.

In one of Fiona Macleod's stories, an old woman named Giorsal lost her daughter Ealàsaidh ('Elsie') to the fairies. Elsie's dreams had been haunted by a fierce monk who threatened her with death because she was a heathen.

Stone pit, Port Beul Mòr. A store for fishing tackle?

John Maclean's House.

After consulting a wise woman near Fionnphort on Mull she took to meeting fairies in the moonlight between Sgéur Iolaire and Cnoc Druidean, an area off-limits to the monks because they once burned a woman there who turned out to be not human. Elsie took to the wilds around the 'Ruins' at Laraichean and was last seen laughing and talking madly in the swampy area at Staonaig. The story is presented as truth and the timescale is presumably late nineteenth century but there is no island tradition of this tale, so it is probably another one of Fiona's fictions. Netta Fornario was known to have been very interested in the 'Ruins' and may have been trying to reach them on the night of her death. I cannot but wonder if she had read Macleod's tale.

THE WEST COAST

The southwest coast has a series of caves (uamh, pronounced 'weem') with varying degrees of accessibility: be prepared for some adventurous exploring. The first, small cave is Uamh a'chroisein, 'Cave of the little cross', at NM 263231. Immediately south is the most famous cave: Uamh an t-Seididh, 'Cave of the blowing', known as the Spouting Cave. Rough seas at half tide causes a spectacular jet of water to burst out of a blowhole. Fiona Macleod names the shore here as the home of 'the Mar-Tarbh, dread creature of the sea'. Just to the south again is Uamh a'Bhodaich, 'Cave of the old man', little more than an overhang, and supposedly where the sheep-stealer of the Cnoc na h-Anatach story was discovered.

Five hundred metres further along the coast is Uamh nan sgarbh, 'Cormorants' Cave', and then Uamh Mhartainn, 'St Martin's Cave', in a gully covered at high tide. The big rock in the sea just to the south is Eilean Maol Mhartuinn, 'the island of the Devotee or Servant of Martin'. All the caves are interesting but whatever traditions were attached to them and their names have now been lost. The oblong stone-lined pit in the pebble beach at the head of Port Beul Mòr may have held fishing tackle, although no one knows for sure.

THE PATH TO COLUMBA'S BAY

This well-trodden but muddy path starts on the machair before climbing south through a landscape of rock and bog. As you start, on your left (to the east) is a hill called Cnoc nan Druidean, but once again the Gaelic name, which seems to suggest Druids, is a false friend, as it means 'Hill of the Starlings'. In a hole in the rocks of Staonaig lived the glaistig. A libation was poured out for her on a stone every night. One very wet day she entered the house of a woman called Livingstone and, finding the woman eating dinner alone, the glaistig held her own garments in front of the fire to dry, but they caught fire. So no female Livingstone can now succeed in kindling a fire at dinner-time. This tale is in Donaldson (1927). At Loch Staonaig you can see remains of the turf dyke (marked as 'Old Wall' on the Colin Baxter map) which stretches from coast to coast. This is the Gàradh Dubh, 'the black wall'; a tradition the origin of which I cannot trace claims it is the border between the 'Christian' north and the 'pagan' south. Other remnants of a vanished agricultural use of the land can be found in the remains of both-ies or shelters for herdsmen at NM 261221 on the east slope of Maol nan Uan (150m southwest of Loch Staonaig) as well as the ruins of houses at the top of the valley leading down to Columba's Bay, Gàradh Eachain Oig ('Enclosure of Hector Og') to the east and Buaile Staoinaig ('Cattlefold of Staoinaig', shown as 'John Maclean's House' on the Baxter map) to the west. All these dwellings were abandoned by the mid nineteenth century at the latest. Trenholme's *The Story of Iona* (1909) relates the history of John Maclean as set out in "Lord Archibald Campbell's book of Argyllshire stories". John fought at Culloden on the losing Jacobite side. When the redcoats came to Iona looking for him a MacInnes boy warned the man and they hid together in an (unnamed) cave until the refugee could escape. The same boy, when an old man, would tell of a cave so large it could hold the entire population of the island, but he would not reveal its location. MacArthur (2001) says John Maclean held the lease from 1738 to 1757 but spent three months in a London prison in 1747, not for fighting at Culloden but for piloting a Jacobite ship to Barra. He had given himself up at Inverary after hiding first in the house and then in the unidentified cave. Southwest of John's house is another stone hut-ring, with a second on a knoll further east past Clach Staoin, a large boulder seemingly balanced on a smaller one.

Pebble Celtic cross and labyrinth at Columba's Bay. The labyrinth design is ancient and can be found in many places, such as on the floor of Chartres Cathedral.

Columba's Bay. St Columba and pilgrim?

COLUMBA'S BAY***

The end destination of the path south, a bay of great beauty, a place of pilgrimage, and the focus of more legends and traditions than you can throw a copy of *The Big Book of Fibs and Fictions* at. The bay is actually in two parts, divided by a central outcrop of rock. The eastern beach, NM 262217, is Port a'Churaich, 'Port of the Curragh', a curragh or curachan being the boat that brought Columba and his twelve companions to here, supposedly their landfall on Iona. As with many of the traditions associated with Columba's Bay, this dates only from the eighteenth century. Adomnan does not mention the landing site (nor does any other authority), so it could have been here, but there is no evidence either way. Towards the head of this part of the bay is a low grass-covered mound 22m long and 7.5m across. Many visitors and Columba-philes have claimed down the years that this marks where Columba's boat was buried. There were once two stone pillars, which marked the stern and prow, and a lesser mound nearby was said to be the smaller boat the curragh carried astern. The less romantic truth, revealed by excavations in 1878 and 1897, is that the mound is natural, probably an isolated portion of storm-beach. Just to the north-north-east is Tobar Glac a'choilich, 'The well at the dell of the cock'. MacArthur (1995) mentions a ringing rock somewhere in the area. Over the years the bay has become a kind of open-air sculpture park for

The cairns on Port an Fhir-Bhreige, possibly raised by medieval pilgrims.

beach-pebble artworks. Some have been there so long they are almost semi-permanent. Others change every year. Labyrinths and Celtic crosses remain popular themes, but I've also seen dolphins, human figures and letters.

The western part of Columba's Bay (NM 263219) is Port an Fhir-Bhreige, 'Port of the false man', supposedly named after a stone that looks like a man, although I have struggled to find this simulacrum. Perhaps it is only visible from the sea. But what is obvious is one of the strangest sights on Iona – at least fifty cairns made of beach pebbles. Most are relatively small – between 1m and 3m in diameter by 0.2m to 0.5m high – but two are much larger, being about 6m across by 1.6m high and surrounded by ditches 1m broad. These cairns are not prehistoric and nothing to do with agriculture. Trenholme (1909) sees them as the cemetery of the men who lived in Port Laraichean to the west. But they are not graves. Pennant (1774) thinks they were erected by monks as a penance. Maxwell (1857) goes one better and surmises the penitents were under obligation to the Druids, and 'If the heaps were proportioned to individual cases of delinquency, then, among them must have been sinners of the deepest dye'. The best guess is that they were constructed as a devotional act by the many pilgrims who came to Iona in medieval times. Here is a good place to look for waterworn pebbles of green Iona marble, long thought to be a talisman against various evils and misfortunes. According to

The 'Ruins' at Laraichean. Not the original Columban settlement or a medieval church, but abandoned stock enclosures and a bothy.

Donaldson (1927) Ionans do not need them as they are immune from drowning, but they grant visitors immunity if worn. They are sometimes called St Columba's Stones or the Mermaid's Tears (see Chapter 2), although Swire describes them as the congealed blood of the Sea-gods. Modern pilgrims are often encouraged to gather two pebbles – one to take home as a reminder of the grace and wonder of Iona, and the second to cast into the sea as a symbol of the letting go of that which is negative and unnecessary.

LARAICHEAN

Further to the west is Uamh na Caisge, 'Cave of Easter', and then at NM 261219 the boat landing of Port Lathraichean or Laraichean. On a terrace above it, in a valley enclosed on three sides, can be found a dyke and the low walls and stone heaps of several ruined buildings. Laraichean means 'foundations' or 'ruins' and many writers have seen this as an ancient or medieval settlement, even going so far as claiming it as the original Columban settlement of 565. Maxwell identifies one of the ruins as that of a church. Once again, the truth is more prosaic: these are post-medieval stock enclosures and an associated bothy, abandoned before the middle of the nineteenth century. As reported in Peter Underwood's *Gazetteer of Scottish Ghosts,* Tommy Frankland was with two nuns on the high headland between Port Laraichean and Port an Fhir-Bhreige when, looking in the direction of Laraichean, they all saw three columns of smoke coming from a deserted spot, with the smoke rising to some twenty feet. Despite extensive investigations, no explanation was forthcoming. One of the nuns said it was the most extraordinary thing she had ever seen.

CARN CULL RI EIRINN, 'THE CAIRN WITH ITS BACK TO IRELAND'

One of the stories that everyone knows about Columba is that, when he arrived at Port a'Churaich, he climbed the nearest hill to see if he could see his beloved Ireland; as he could not, and therefore would not be tempted to return, he pronounced Iona a suitable place for his monastery. And he called the viewpoint Carn Cull ri Eirinn, 'the Cairn with its back to Ireland'. The story is neat, poignant, backed up by place names – and entirely fictional. Adomnan does not mention it, and neither do any of the ancient or medieval writers; its earliest recorded reference is in the eighteenth century, the era when Columban stories were being promulgated by, or for the benefit of, distinguished visitors. Donaldson (1927) is the only writer I can trace who claims another Carn Cull ri Eirinn on a hill behind the Nunnery. There are definitely other Carn Cull ri Eirinns on Mull and Colonsay, as well as placenames meaning 'Cairn with its back to Alba',

Alba being the west coast of the Scottish mainland; this has led historians to suggest these various cairns may have marked a cultural or political boundary between peoples who held allegiance to either Ireland or Alba. And, to top it all, if you climb the hill Carn Cull ri Eirinn (NM 258223) on a clear day, you can see...Ireland.

THE SOUTHEAST COAST

This part of Iona is rough going and very boggy. The old marble quarry down a steep gully to the coast at NM 269220 has interesting industrial relics. One hundred and fifty metres north is the ruined Tobhta nan Sasunnaich, 'the house of the lowlanders', presumably the quarry workers. The Ritchies' 1928 map shows Sithean mor na h-aird, 'the Big Fairy Mound of the Aird' immediately north of the quarry, although I have not been able to identify it. This Sithean may be connected with the story of Dugald and his lethal fairy sweetheart, told in MacArthur (1990): the story was recorded in 1963 by Donald MacFarlane of Deargphort in the Ross of Mull, who heard it from his father Hector MacFarlan, and who in turn was told it by the old folk when he worked in Iona as a boy. Because Dugald had a fairy sweetheart, a smith made him a steel arrow as protection, which he had to carry at all times. But he was to be best man at a wedding one day and changed out of his normal clothes. He went to hunt rabbits until the wedding began but he never returned. His body was found next day. The fairy, jealous of the human bride, jealous of the dancing and joy, and upset that she could not persuade her human lover to join her in the Otherworld, had killed him. Frank Delaney, in *A Walk to The Western Isles,* adds the details that his face was 'strewn with petals, the torso covered with bright seashells' and the body was found 'in a grassy hollow by the shore', although the usual site mentioned is the high ground named after Dugald, Druim Dhùghaill, some 700m to the north of the quarry. South of Druim Dhùghaill is Uamh nan Calman, 'Pigeons' Cave', a double hole where naturalist Henry Graham stole eggs and shot his way through the island's bird population in the 1850s, and 500m further north, the small Sloc a'Gharaidh Ghil, 'Gully of the White Den', usually called Otters' Cave. Fiona Macleod (*Iona*) recounts falling asleep on Sliav Starr and dreaming of the Divine Forges, where three great blacksmith-spirits rescued souls from the depths, recast them and fitted them with wings on a giant anvil, and then set them free through star-gateways. In the wilderness on the east side of the valley from Cnoc nan Druidean, west of Maol nam Manach, and south of the end of track that leads past Ruanaich, is Creag Ghrugach, 'Frowning rock', another simulacrum of a face. A gruagach is also a supernatural creature, often a guardian spirit of cattle.

9

STAFFA

I have seen the temple not made with hands.

Sir Robert Peel, from a speech in Glasgow,
13 January 1837

Staffa's isle, where Nature scoffs at Art!

Anonymous poem, in James Johnson,
The Recess (1834)

Thro' darken'd domes and dens of wonder,
And caverns of eternal thunder!

Sir Walter Scott, *The Lord of the Isles*

THE ISLAND

Staffa can be reached by boat-trip from Iona or Mull. With its thousands of geo-
metrical black basalt columns formed by volcanic activity, and the amazing Fingal's
Cave, it is a natural wonder, matched geologically with the Giant's Causeway in
Northern Ireland. The island is uninhabited. Note that rough seas may inhibit
landing and most commercial boat visits allow the visitor only a limited number
of hours ashore.

LEGENDS

All the island's creation legends feature giants. Torquil MacLeod of Eigg carried
the best piece of the Giant's Causeway with him in a sack as he waded home.
A few fragments fell out – forming the small rocks southwest of Staffa – and
then the entire sack split, and Staffa splashed into the sea. It had been a long day,
so Torquil, tired and grumpy, left it where it was. A nine-headed monster used
the great cave to preserve his victims in vinegar and malt whisky before eating
them. Fingal (Fionn mac Cumhail/Finn McCool) in his giant guise built both
Staffa and the Giant's Causeway so he could walk to Scotland to fight his Scottish

Left: Map of Staffa.

Opposite: Illustration from Barthelemy Faujas de Saint Fond's *A Journey Through England and Scotland to the Hebrides in 1784* in which Fingal's Cave has been transformed into a regular-sided *über-*temple.

equivalent Benandonner. There is a persistent legend that the two sites are connected, either by a tunnel or a causeway immediately under the surface of the sea. In some versions this gigantiform infrastructure is inhabited by the Fionn, or by giants, or by other mythical peoples. Fingal and his giantess wife sheltered a storm-bound monk in the cave; he told them of the Gospels, and eventually they were converted to Christianity. When they first entered the church on Iona they had to do so on their hands and knees, but when Columba finished saying Mass the couple were of normal size.

Fingal was not always a giant; mostly he was the main character in a series of Irish hero tales, in which he and his warband the Feinne/Fionn – think Arthur and the Knights of the Round Table, only with no Christian overlay – engaged in adventures of love, war, betrayal, hunting and supernatural derring-do. These myths are well-known across Ireland and Gaelic Scotland, and have left their mark on hundreds of placenames and features. The *Ossian* poems, claimed to be the work of Ossian, a third-century bard and Fingal's son, were almost certainly the creation of an eighteenthcentury schoolmaster, James MacPherson. Despite the controversy the poems took Europe by storm – Napoleon famously took a copy on campaign with him – and greatly increased the popularity of Fingalian stories outside Gaeldom. Fingal the giant may have built Staffa and excavated Fingal's Cave, but it is Fingal the hero who feasted in the Cave with his warriors and bards. Stories, however, have a tendency to mutate. In the early twentieth century, when Donald MacCulloch asked people on neighbouring islands about

Fingal's Cave, he was told Fingal was a great pirate who plundered the west coast, hid his treasure on Staffa and kept his galley in the cave.

A story of pagan gods, divine magic, sex-punishment and mermaids has latched onto the real-life Abbot MacKinnon of Iona (d.1498), whose effigy and cross can be seen in the Abbey. The best-known version is *The Abbot MacKinnon,* by James Hogg (1770-1835), part of his 1813 poetry collection *The Queen's Wake.* The story is apparently based on an old Hebridean legend. The Abbot, having broken his vow of celibacy with Matilda of Skye, was visited by Columba in a dream. The saint − here behaving more as a pagan than a Christian − had vowed to the sea and the sun that recompense for sins would be paid to the god of the waters (possibly Manannan again?) Gathering other monks who had sinned carnally, MacKinnon sailed to Staffa. The penitents burned incense and prayed for forgiveness in Fingal's Cave, but a loud supernatural voice said, 'Greater yet must the offering be'. Crossing over to western side of the island, the monks looked down into Port an Fhasgaid and saw a mermaid singing of the righteous retribution they must suffer. In despair they rushed back to the boat at Clamshell Cave, to find a strange old man with a long grey beard sitting in the bow, chanting, 'Oh, woe is me, but great as the sin but the sacrifice be'. Something about him reminded MacKinnon of Columba. The monks pushed off but were caught in a storm, at which moment the old man rose up, raised his hands and cried, 'Now is the time'. All were immediately drowned by a squall (so who survived to tell the tale?)

FANTASY AND IMAGINATION

Staffa first became widely known after the naturalist Sir Joseph Banks described it in 1772 in *The Scots Magazine* and elsewhere. Soon intrepid travellers were setting out – in difficult and dangerous conditions – to see this 'awe-ful' sight on the edge of the world. Inaccurate and exaggerated descriptions and pictorial representations circulated. In some cases the exaggeration may have been intentional, designed to fire the Georgian imagination with images of both the Sublime and the Grotesque. As Donald MacCulloch notes (*Staffa,* 1927): 'During those early days, before the cold logic of science had given a clear explanation of its formation, Staffa was invested with a much more mystical and dreadful atmosphere than it is now'. However, that is no excuse for an astonishing piece of hyperbole, a small pamphlet first published in London in 1791 and frequently reprinted thereafter, entitled: *A Description of the Curious Monuments and Antiquities in the Island of Icolmkill, or the Island of St Colman-kill [Iona]; also an account of the Island of Staffa, where the rural throne of the late King Fingal is extant; being the Chief of the Heroes, so much admired by the Poets. By a Gentleman who made the Tour of Europe, prior to this Description, in a letter to a Friend. It is now published by the desire of several Gentlemen of Distinction who reside in the Country; and given to the bearer, John McCormick, upon account of his misfortunes, to help him to support a small family.* Staffa is 'supported upon pillars in the middle of the ocean; the pillars are of a mixed marble, and no marble containing such a variety of brilliant colours was ever discovered in Britain….the subterraneous part thereof is so naturally arched and decorated, that it exceeds the most exquisite performance of the greatest artists in the world. There is a melodious cave on the island; any music played or sunk therein will in reality have a sound more melodious than an organ. The rocks towards the sea seem as if they were polished by artists of great taste; the pebbles on the shore have every appearance of beautiful pearls…at the distance of a league, when passing the same [cave] in dark nights, a visible sparkling like diamonds will cast a lustre at a great distance. On the top of the island there is a beautiful natural seat of marble, resembling an easy chair, which is said to be King Fingal's throne, and contiguous thereto there are three pyramids resembling a sugar loaf, which beautifies the royal seat'. It was perhaps panegyrics such as this that tempted a man who turned up at Ulva and asked to be ferried to Staffa to sail in and out between the marble pillars. When told the columns were massed together and were black rock not marble he simply packed up and went home.

The sheer majesty and apparently baffling nature of the island's features prompted a number of idiosyncratic responses. In *The Scottish Geographical Magazine* of October 1887, Cope Whitehouse, in an essay called 'The Caves of Staffa', set out his theory that Staffa was a fortress built by refugees from the Mediterranean civilisations to protect Iona, the beacon of learning. The caves were all man-made, the excavation starting from the top, with the columns then loosened and extracted through the holes. The caves were shelters and hiding places for the long Phoenician galleys, breakwaters being built to protect the entrance of each cave. A fire beacon in Fingal's Cave would warn Iona of approaching invaders. In Comyns Beaumont's 1946 book *The Riddle of Prehistoric Britain,* Staffa and other basaltic rock formations are the remnants of a comet which struck or grazed the earth in 1322 BC, travelling northeast to southwest across the north of Europe and Britain. The impact caused the Earth's axis to wobble, and, via the real biblical flood, the destruction of Atlantis, which was centred on Scandinavia and Britain. The scattered survivors made their way south and founded the civilisations of Greece, Phoenicia, the Holy Land and Egypt. The Greek orders of capitals for columns – Ionian, Doric and Corinthian – were based on memories of Staffa's columns. Fingal's Cave was the original Judgement Hall of Amenti (mentioned in the *Egyptian Book of the Dead*) where Osiris judged the souls of the dead. Even the Devil gets a look in, being the nucleus of the comet, which is buried under Staffa. The ancient astronomers observed the comet with its fiery tail and small horn-like protrusions from the head, and named it Satan. For corroboration Beaumont references Luke 10.18 – 'I beheld Satan as lightning fall from heaven' – and the Roman writer Plutarch, who says Satan was cast down from the sky deep into a burning region beneath the sea, and covered by an island of fiery rocks and stones which lay at the ends of the earth. Further, old Greek and Roman stories have Hell in the northern parts of the British Isles. The now-forgotten Beaumont (1873-1956) was a thoroughgoing English eccentric who combined journalism for the *Daily Mail* with writing batty books about Pharaohs ruling South Wales and Edinburgh as the original Jerusalem. This was his third book of this stripe, a furrow he was plough-ing decades before Velikovsky's *Worlds in Collision* made the Catastrophist school of thought famous. With its familiar obsession with ancient civilisations and strikes from space, its cavalier disregard for the historical and archaeological record, and its appetite for twisting quotations and authorities to meet its own pre-determined conclusions, *The Riddle of Prehistoric Britain* seems strangely modern.

Others had more spiritual concerns. Clearly concerned by the rise of science and the questioning of biblical and religious authority, an anonymous aristocrat saw Staffa as clear proof of the existence of God. His poem, published in the early nineteenth century in the *Metropolitan Magazine* and reprinted in 1834 in James Johnson's *The Recess, or Autumnal Relaxation in the Highlands and Lowlands,* ends:

> …*Who, while he views the loveliness of earth,*
> *Can yet disown the power that gave it birth –*
> *Here let him gaze, and say 'twas chance alone,*
> *That rear's the pile and nicely carved the stone,*
> *That lent each shaft such noble symmetry –*
> *Alas! It mocks his poor philosophy,*
> *Suggests a truth he little dreamt before –*
> *Man was not made to question, but adore!*

A visitor thought The Herdsman was the heap of columns that had been excavated from Fingal's Cave, or perhaps the builder's job-lot of surplus columns left over after Staffa had been finished.

A TOUR OF THE ISLAND

This tour starts at the landing place at Clamshell Cave and proceeds clockwise around the coast. Note many of the caves are dangerous, some accessible only at low tide, and others only by boat. To visit all the sites you will need more time than the average commercial boat-trip allows.

CLAMSHELL (OR SCALLOP) CAVE ***

The columns at this incredible place are bent into a formation like a clamshell or the ribs of a wooden ship. The opposite north side appears like a giant honey-comb. The small rock of columns in the sea just to the south is Am Brachial, 'The Herdsman', the narrow passage between which and Staffa is often taken up by fast-racing tidal bores. John Stoddard, who visited in 1799, noted The Herdsman was said to consist of 8,000 distinct stones on each of which stood one of the Feinne.

THE CAUSEWAY***

This is the route south to Fingal's Cave, past the Bending Columns, which do what they say on the can. In the cliff is a seat-like recess called Fingal's Wishing Chair, although this name may be quite modern – in 1816 a German visitor, the splendidly-named Dr Spiker, did not use the name and instead called it The Priest, supposed to be the site of a former altar. To ensure your wish will be fulfilled, the procedure is to sit, wish silently and keep the wish private. One lady asked her fellow visitors if the wishes came true. A gentleman said they did, as he had proved on several visits to Staffa. What was his wish? 'On each occasion I wished I would get safely back to Oban?'

FINGAL'S CAVE***

What an enchanted place this Fingal's Cave is! Who could be so dull of soul as not to believe that it was created by a god for sylphs and water-nymphs!

Jules Verne, *The Green Ray*

The 70m-long sea cave, formed entirely of hexagonal basalt columns, is magnificent. Try to visit alone if you can – it is like being inside a cathedral of stone, only with the boom of waves. You can find yourself believing – as described in another part of the anonymous poem mentioned above – that this is the abode of the kraken, the greatest sea monster of them all. One of the strange experiences of the cave is that if you venture deep inside along the crude walkway and look out, on a clear day you can see Iona Abbey – the two are aligned perfectly, and the framing cave entrance somehow allows a clearer view than from the rest of the island.

The almost-universal opinion is that the name comes from the Irish hero/ giant Fingal, as noted above, but there are two other suggestions: that it is a corruption of the Gaelic for 'musical cave', *uamh bhinn*, pronounced 'oo-a-veen', close to the way Fionn is sometimes pronounced; or that it is derived from the Gaelic for Danish Vikings, *Fionn-ghoill*, 'white or fair foreigners'. The name Staffa is itself Norse. So far, the jury is out, but Fingal is ahead by a sword's breadth.

The cave was a temple of Romanticism, and attracted romantics of both big 'R' and small 'r' persuasions. When Sir Walter Scott visited in July 1810 the boatmen christened a stone at the mouth of the cavern Clachan-an-Bhaird ('the Poet's Stone'). There was an extended oration in Gaelic followed by a pibroch and, inevitably, whisky. Jules Verne visited in 1859 and set the climax of his 1882 novel *The Green Ray* on Staffa. The eponymous light is a legendary flash which appears just as the sun sinks into the sea. Whoever witnesses it makes no mistakes in love. The heroine sees it, rejects her frigid suitor, and chooses the dashing hero who saves her from a storm in Fingal's Cave. In real life they would have perished within minutes. *Fingal's Cave*, Mendolssohn's overture to *The Hebrides*, is just one of the musical responses to the setting. In 1886 the string band of the PS *Chevalier* were towed into the cave to perform The Old Hundredth and the national anthem to an audience of hats-off tourists. On 10 June 1897, a group of eminent clergymen who had just been on Iona to mark the 1300th anniversary of Columba's death gathered in the cave and, very impressively, sang the 103rd Psalm. You can imagine the effect. The sounds of bagpipes, pistols and foghorns have been tried out. A Miss Barker of Cumberland, who spent two days and nights on Staffa in August 1928, found the initials 'J.B. 1772' cut into a column at the very inner end of the cave, in a place difficult to access. The letters are two inches high and very weathered. Could it be a practical joke, or did Sir Joseph Banks really graffiti the cave? A memorial stone in a glass container was hidden in a secret spot within the cave in 1900; it is probably still there.

THE COLONNADE ***

Also known as the Great Face, these sheer cliffs of columns – only visible from a boat – are suggestive of the façade of a Greek temple. Around the end of the Second World War a floating mine exploded against the Colonnade and destroyed many columns just outside the west entrance to Fingal's Cave. Boat Cave, just to the west of the Colonnade, appears from the sea to be nothing remarkable, but if entered by boat (the only access) it proves to be over 40m long, with smooth yellow walls and a roof composed of apparently unsupported columns.

MACKINNON'S CAVE **

This is almost as large and impressive as Fingal's Cave, being more than 65m long, with a remarkable hood of columns over the entrance and a flat ceiling-like roof. Although it can be entered on foot at low tide it is a perilous route as the cave is exposed to the full force of the Atlantic. The best way in is through the passage from Cormorants' Cave at the back, which takes you from the winding darkness to the overpowering vastness of MacKinnon's Cave. A tradition relating to the name has Abbot MacKinnon leaving Iona following some religious dispute and sheltering his boat here. The shelter was inadequate (or the many seabirds too noisy) so he sailed for Mull, finding home in a cave at Gribun. On the other hand, the MacKinnon clan originated on Mull and were closely associated with Iona in the fifteenth century, so it is not surprising to find their name on local features.

CORMORANTS' CAVE **

From the sea this just looks like a narrow slit but in fact it extends for almost 20m, and can be approached at low tide. An opening to the right at the end takes you through a winding tunnel into MacKinnon's Cave. Bring a torch.

Staffa, showing (right to left) Fingal's Cave, the Colonnade and MacKinnon's Cave.

GUNNA MOR, 'THE BIG GUN'**

To the north of Port an Fhasgaidh – the bay where the doomed monks saw the mermaid – is another natural wonder, a 'pipe' in the cliff as regular and smooth as the bore of a cannon running upwards steeply at forty-five degrees. Murray (1802) describes a probably fictitious story of a loose boulder being driven up and down the 'gun' by storms, making a sound like thunder; the stone was apparently stolen by Irish souvenir hunters many years earlier. To the northwest and northeast of the island are two small sea-caves, neither of them notable.

THE RUINS

The centre of the island has a single ruin. For many years it was thought to be the remains of a medieval chapel or hermit's cell, but it is now regarded as a projected hostel for visitors, or a folly, built between 1815-1820 but never completed. It is not one of the huts of the last inhabitants. De Saint Fond, who visited in 1784, described two families, filthy and lice-ridden, who lived in great poverty. Fourteen years later Professor T. Garnett, in *A Tour through the Highlands of Scotland*, said a herdsman and his family now only spent the summers on the island. They formerly lived there all year round but one stormy winter they left, because the pot which hung over the fire vibrated in the storm, and 'nothing but an evil spirit could have rocked it in that manner'.

APPENDIX
SOME NOTES ON IONA AND STAFFA IN POPULAR CULTURE

The role-playing computer game *Summoner* is set in a magical quasi-medieval world rife with demons, magicians and other fantasy entities. Among its many exotic locations is the 'mysterious monastery on the Isle of Iona'.

The Scottish band Iona use a combination of classic rock, prog, ambient and Scottish/Irish folk approaches to tell stories of Christian and Gaelic spirituality, often with specific references to Iona. The American group Sleeping Kings of Iona create a Sigur Ros type sound, which although having nothing to do with Iona directly, has a suitably mysterious quality to it. Perhaps the best-known Iona-related songs in popular music are Mike Scott's 'Iona Song' on *Bring 'Em All In* and 'Peace of Iona' on *Universal Hall* by Scott's group The Waterboys.

Holy Terror in the Hebrides by Jeanne M. Dams is a 'cosy' murder mystery set on Iona and Staffa, with an intrepid female American expatriate up against a sinister religious group.

St Columba features as a minor character in the *Swamp Thing* series of comics/graphic novels. He has become a member of the cosmically-wise group of Earth Elementals known as the Parliament of Trees. And Columba, Oran and Iona have a grim role to play in another comic/graphic novel, *Empathy is the Enemy,* one of the consistently dark *Hellblazer* stories featuring the troubled wide-boy magus John Constantine.

BIBLIOGRAPHY

The works I have found the most useful are marked with an asterisk★.

HISTORY, ARCHAEOLOGY AND RELIGION – IONA AND STAFFA

Alexander, Revd W. Lindsay *Iona,* The Religious Tract Society, London 1850.

Anderson, Alan Orr & Marjorie Ogilvie Anderson (ed. and trans.) *Adomnan's Life of Columba,* Thomas Nelson & Sons, London 1961.★

Argyll, 8th Duke of *Iona,* Daniel Mackay, Oban 1913 (first published 1870).

Bourke, Cormac (ed.) *Studies in the Cult of Saint Columba,* Four Courts Press, Dublin 1997.

Broun, Dauvit and Thomas Owen Clancy (eds.) *Spes Scotorum: Hope of Scots,* T. & T. Clark, Edinburgh 1999.★

Clancy, Thomas Owen 'Columba, Adomnan and the cult of saints in Scotland' in Broun and Clancy (eds.) *Spes Scotorum: Hope of Scots.*

Clancy, Thomas Owen and Gilbert Márkus *Iona: The Earliest Poetry of a Celtic Monastery,* Edinburgh University Press, Edinburgh 2003.★

De Watteville, Alastair *Staffa,* Romsey Fine Art, Romsey 1993.

———— *The Isle of Iona,* Romsey Fine Art, Romsey 1999.

Drummond, James *Sculptured Monuments in Iona & The West Highlands,* Society of Antiquaries of Scotland, Edinburgh 1881.★

Dunbar, John G. and Ian Fisher *Iona: A Guide to the Monuments,* HMSO, Edinburgh 1995.★

Ewing, Bishop Alexander *The Cathedral or Abbey Church of Iona and the Early Celtic Church and Mission of St Columba,* R. Grant & Son, Edinburgh 1866.

Ferguson, Malcolm *A Trip From Callander to Staffa and Iona,* John Leng & Co. (Dundee) and Macniven and Wallace (Edinburgh) 1894.

Finlay, Ian *Columba,* Gollancz, London 1979.

Hannan, Thomas *Iona: and Some Satellites,* W. & R. Chambers, London 1929

Graham, H.D. *Antiquities of Iona,* Day & Son, London 1850.

Huyshe, Wentworth *The Life of St Columba,* London 1905.

Jamieson, John *A Historical Account of the Ancient Culdees of Iona,* Thomas D. Morison (Glasgow) and Simpkin, Marshall, Hamilton & Co. (London) 1890.

MacArthur, E. Mairi *Iona: The Living Memory of a Crofting Community 1750-1914,* Edinburgh University Press, Edinburgh 1990.★

———— *Columba's Island: Iona from Past to Present,* Edinburgh University Press, Edinburgh 1995.★

———— *Iona,* Colin Baxter Photography, Grantown-on-Spey 2001.★

MacCulloch, Donald B. *Staffa,* David and Charles, Newton Abbott 1975 (first edition 1927).★

MacLeod, the Very Revd George F. *Come Around With Me: Short Tour of Iona Abbey,* Iona Community, Glasgow (no date).

MacMillan & Brydell, *Iona: Its History, Antiquities etc.* 1898.

McNeill, F. Marion (ed.) *An Iona Anthology,* The Iona Community, Glasgow 1952.★

McNeill, F. Marion *Iona A History of the Island,* Lochar Publishing, Moffat 1991 (first edition 1920).★

MacPhail, J.R.N. 'The Cleansing of I-colum-cille' in *Scottish Historical Review Vol. 22* 1925.

Marsden, John *The Illustrated Life of Columba,* Floris Books, Edinburgh 1995.★

Mathers, Ewan *The Cloisters of Iona Abbey,* Wild Goose Publications, Glasgow 2001.★

Maxwell, W. *Iona and the Ionians,* Thomas Murray and Son, Glasgow 1857.★

Meek, Donald E. 'Between faith and folklore: twentieth-century interpretations and images of Columba', in Broun and Clancy (eds.) *Spes Scotorum: Hope of Scots*★

Meehan, Bernard *The Book of Kells,* Thames & Hudson, London 1994.

Menzies, Lucy *St Columba of Iona: A Short Account of His Life,* The Iona Community, Glasgow 1949.

New Statistical Account of Scotland, 'Parish of Kilfinichen and Kilviceuen' Vol. VII, Edinburgh 1845.

O'Donnell, Manus (ed. Brian Lacey) *The Life of Colum Cille,* Four Courts Press, Dublin 1998 (written 1532).★

O'Sullivan, Jerry 'Excavation of an Early Church and a Women's Cemetery at St Ronan's Medieval Parish Church, Iona' in *Proceedings of the Royal Society of Antiquaries in Scotland* Vol. 124, National Museums of Scotland, Edinburgh 1994.

———— 'Iona: archaeological investigations, 1875-1996' in Broun and Clancy (eds.) *Spes Scotorum: Hope of Scots.*★

Old Statistical Account of Scotland, 'Parish of Kilfinichen and Kilviceuen' vol. XIV, Edinburgh 1795.

Reeves, W. (ed.) *Adamnan's St Columba; text and notes* 1857; re-edited by William Skene, Edinburgh 1874.

Ritchie, Alec and Euphemia *Iona Past and Present with Maps,* Highland Home Industries, Edinburgh 1947 (first edition 1928).★

Ritchie, Anna *Iona,* B.T. Batsford/Historic Scotland, London 1997.★

Ritchie, Anna and Ian Fisher, *Iona Abbey and Nunnery,* Historic Scotland, Edinburgh 2003.★

Royal Commission on Ancient and Historical Monuments in Scotland *Argyll: An Inventory of the Monuments* Vol. 4: *Iona,* HMSO, Edinburgh 1982.★

Sacheverell, William *An Account of the Isle of Man with a Voyage to I-Columb-Kill in the Year 1688* (ed. Revd J.G. Cumming), The Manx Society, Douglas 1859 (first published 1702).★

Smith, John *The Life of Columba, the Apostle and Patron Saint of the Ancient Scots and Picts,* Mundell & Son, Glasgow 1798.

Steer, K.A. & W.M. Bannerman *Late Medieval Sculpture in the West Highlands,* Royal Commission on Ancient and Historical Monuments in Scotland, Edinburgh 1977.★

Trenholme, E.C. *The Story of Iona,* David Douglas, Edinburgh 1909.

HISTORY, ARCHAEOLOGY AND RELIGION – SCOTLAND AND IRELAND

Airlie, Stuart 'The View From Maastricht' in Crawford, Barbara E (ed.) *Scotland in Dark Age Europe* 1994.

Alcock, Leslie *Kings and Warriors, Craftsmen and Priests* Society of Antiquaries of Scotland Monograph Series, Edinburgh 2003.

Boswell, James *The Journal of a Tour to the Hebrides, with Samuel Johnson,* Oxford University Press, Oxford 1970 (first published 1785).

Burl, Aubrey *Stone Circles of the British Isles,* Yale University Press, Newhaven and London 1977.

Crawford, Barbara E. (ed.) *Scotland in Dark Age Europe*, St John's House Papers No. 5, The Committee for Dark Ages Studies, University of St Andrews, St Andrews 1994.

De Saint Fond, Barthelemy Faujas *A Journey Through England and Scotland to the Hebrides in 1784*, Hugh Hopkins, Glasgow 1907 (first published 1797).

Delaney, Frank *A Walk to The Western Isles After Boswell and Johnson,* HarperCollins, London 1993.

Donaldson, M.E.M., *Wanderings in the Western Highlands and Islands,* Alexander Gardner, Paisley 1927.★

Douglas, Ronald MacDonald *The Scots Book,* Senate, Twickenham 1995 (original edition 1949).

Gordon, Revd J.F.S. *Ecclesiastical Chronicle for Scotland: Monasticon,* James MacVeigh, London 1875.

Gordon, Seton *Afoot in the Hebrides,* Country Life, London 1950.

Gunn, Neil *Off In A Boat,* Richard Drew Publishing, Glasgow 1988 (first published 1938).

James, David *Celtic Art: The Carved Stones of Western Scotland, a Guide and Inspiration,* The Thule Press 1979.

Johnson, Samuel *A Journey to the Western Isles of Scotland,* Oxford University Press, Oxford 1970 (first published 1775).

Logan, James *The Scottish Gael; or, Celtic Manners as Preserved Among the Highlanders* 2 vols, Smith, Elder & Co, London 1831.

McDonald, R. Andrew *The Kingdom of the Isles: Scotland's Western Seaboard c. 1100-c.1336,* Tuckwell Press, East Linton 1997

Marsden, John *Sea-Road of the Saints: Celtic Holy Men in the Hebrides,* Floris Books, Edinburgh 1995.★

Martin, Martin *A Description of the Western Isles of Scotland,* Birlinn, Edinburgh 1994 (first published 1703).★

Moffat, Alistair *The Sea Kingdoms: The Story of Celtic Britain and Ireland,* HarperCollins, London 2001.

Monro, Sir Donald, High Dean of the Isles, *A Description of the Western Isles of Scotland,* Birlinn, Edinburgh 1994 (first published 1774).★

Murray, The Hon. Mrs Sarah (of Kensington) *A Companion and Useful Guide to the Beauties in the West Highlands of Scotland and in the Hebrides,* Vol. II London 1803.

Pococke, Bishop Richard *Pococke's Tours in Scotland,* ed. by DW Kemp, Scottish History Society, Vol 1, Edinburgh 1887.★

Robson, Michael (ed.) *Curiosities of Art and Nature: Martin Martin's classic 'A Description of the Western Isles of Scotland',* The Islands Book Trust, Isle of Lewis 2003

Ross, Anne and Don Robins *The Life and Death of a Druid Prince,* Rider, London 1989

Skene, William F., *Celtic Scotland* 3 vols, David Douglas, Edinburgh 1876-1880.★

Smyth, Alfred P. *Warlords and Holy Men: Scotland AD 80-1000,* Edinburgh University Press, Edinburgh 1984.★

Sutherland, Halliday *Hebridean Journey,* Geoffrey, Bles, London 1939.

Walker, Rev. Dr. John *Report on the Hebrides of 1764 and 1771,* (ed. Margaret M. McKay) John Donald Publishers, Edinburgh 1980.

Walsh, J.R. and T. Bradley *A History of the Irish Church 400-700AD,* Dublin 1991.

Williams, Ronald *The Lords of the Isles: The Clan Donald and the early Kingdom of the Scots,* House of Lochar, Isle of Colonsay 1997 (first published 1984).

Wilson, Daniel *Prehistoric Annals of Scotland* 2 vols, MacMillan & Co., London and Cambridge 1863.

MYSTERIOUSNESS

Alexander, Marc *Enchanted Britain,* Arthur Barker, London 1981.

Archibald, Malcolm *Scottish Animal and Bird Folklore,* Saint Andrew Press, Edinburgh 1996.

Balfour, Michael *Mysterious Scotland,* Mainstream, Edinburgh 1997.

Beaumont, Comyns *The Riddle of Prehistoric Britain,* Rider & Co., London, 1946.★

Benham, Patrick *The Avalonians,* Gothic Image Publications, Glastonbury 1993.★

Carmichael, Alexander (ed. C.J. Moore) *Carmina Gadelica* Floris Books, Edinburgh 1994 (first published 1900).★

Costello, Peter *Jules Verne: Inventor of Science Fiction,* Hodder & Stoughton, London 1978.

Ellis, Peter Beresford *Dictionary of Celtic Mythology,* Constable, London 1992.

Fortune, Dion *Psychic Self-Defence,* The Aquarian Press, London 1988.★

Frazer, Sir James George *The Golden Bough,* London 1922.

Green, Miranda *The Gods of the Celts,* Bramley Books, Godalming 1986.

————— *Dictionary of Celtic Myth and Legend,* Thames and Hudson, London 1997.

Harries, John *The Ghost Hunter's Road Book* Frederick Muller, London 1968.

Hawken, Paul *The Magic of Findhorn,* Fontana/Collins, Glasgow 1975.

Hayman, Richard *Riddles in Stone: Myths, Archaeology and the Ancient Britons,* The Hambledon Press, London and Rio Grande, Ohio 1997.

King, Francis *Ritual Magic in England,* New English Library, London 1972.

Lines, Marianna *Sacred Stones Sacred Places,* Saint Andrew Press, Edinburgh 1992.

MacBeth, Ivan, 'Crystal Hunter', 1999, unpublished, online at www.isleofavalon.co.uk/GlastonburyArchive.

MacEowen, Frank 'Odhran: Patron Saint of the Lower World' in DALRIADA: The Journal of Celtic Culture, Heritage & Traditions, Volume 12, Issue Number 2, 1997.

Macleod, Fiona (William Sharp) *The Divine Adventure; Iona; Studies in Spiritual History [By Sundown Shores]* Heinemann, London 1919 (first published 1910).★

————— *The Washer of the Ford: And other Legendary Moralities* Patrick Geddes and Colleagues, Edinburgh 1896.★

McMahon, Joanne and Jack Roberts, *The Sheela-na-Gigs of Ireland and Britain,* Mercier Press, Cork and Dublin 2000.

McNeill, F. Marion *The Silver Bough* Vol. 1: *Scottish Folk-Lore and Folk-Belief,* Canongate, Edinburgh 1989 (First published 1956).

Merry, Eleanor C. *Odrun: The Rune of the Depths,* The Orient-Occident Publishing Co., London 1928.

————— *The Flaming Door (The Mission of the Celtic Folk-Soul,)* Floris Books, Edinburgh 1983.

Perrott, Tom 'A Strange Adventure on the Isle of Iona', in Ghost Trackers Newsletter Vol 10 No 2 June 1991, Chicago.

Spence, Lewis *The Mysteries of Britain* Senate, London 1994 (first published 1905).

Swire, Otta F. *The Inner Hebrides and Their Legends,* Collins, London and Glasgow 1964.★

Tame, David *Real Fairies: True Accounts of Meetings with Nature Spirits,* Capell Bann Publishing, Chieveley 1999.

Thompson, Francis *Ghosts Spirits and Spectres of Scotland,* Langsyne, Newtongrange 1984.

Underwood, Peter *Gazetteer of Scottish Ghosts,* Fontana/Collins, Glasgow 1974.★

Wilson, Richard *Scotland's Unsolved Mysteries of the Twentieth Century,* Robert Hale, London 1989.★

INDEX

Abbey 10, 28, 35, 36, 39, 44, 45, 47-79, 80, 119

An Eala (coffin mound) 29-31, 45

Aidan, King of Dalriada 8, 18, 53

Angels 16-20, 41, 52, 66, 67, 75-77, 88, 96-99

Argyll, Dukes of 10, 48, 54, 65, 66, 83

Atlantis 117

Barnacle Geese 25

Batman 21

Beaumont, Comyns (*The Riddle of Prehistoric Britain)* 117

Black Stones of Iona, The 42, 53-54

Blàr Buidhe cairn 37

Book of Kells, The 59, 61, 63, 73

Boece, Hector 24, 54, 73

Cadell, FCB (artist) 86, 91

Cairns 8, 37, 84, 99, 110

Carmina Gadelica (Alexander Carmichael) 19, 28, 32, 98-100

Carvings and Statues (*see also* Gargoyles and Grotesques) 16, 26, 32, 35, 36, 42, 44, 46, 48, 50-79, 120

Caves 93, 106-107, 111, 112, 114-120

Celtic Gods 82, 92, 100, 115

Clach-Bràth (Day of Judgement Stone) 46, 78-79

Cohea, William H., Jnr 7

Crosses and cross-marked stones 9, 24, 28, 32, 33-34, 36, 37, 42, 44-46, 48, 49, 50-52, 54, 58, 59, 66, 71-72, 76-79, 80, 94, 108, 110

Culdees 10, 12, 90

Curses (*see* Magic)

Customs and rituals 18, 19-20, 39-40, 41, 42, 45, 49, 53-54, 65, 78-79, 83, 87, 98-99

Dalriada 8, 15, 18, 44, 53

Day of Judgement Stone, The (*see* Clach-Bràth)

Demons 18, 21, 39, 41, 65, 91

Divination 22, 23, 28, 49, 56, 78

Dragons and wyverns 35, 55, 56, 57, 61, 62, 63, 71, 75, 76, 77, 79

Dreams (*see* Visions)

Druids 17, 21, 22-23, 39-40, 41, 42, 78, 87-88, 90, 93, 94, 107

Duncan, John (artist) 83, 88, 99

Fairies and other supernatural entities 11, 20, 22-24, 32, 39, 92, 93, 94

Fingal and the Fingalians 37, 113-115, 116, 118, 119

Fornario, Netta Emily (occultist) 45, 101-106

Fortune, Dion (occultist) 103

Funerals 29, 31, 49

Gargoyles and Grotesques (*see also* Carvings) 34, 55, 56-57, 61, 62, 63, 65, 70

Ghosts and hauntings 22, 34, 36, 45, 60, 72, 76, 84-85, 91, 93

Giants 37, 113-114

Glaistig (*see also* Fairies) 107

Graveyards and graveslabs 26, 28, 29-31, 34-35, 36, 38-46, 49, 52, 58-59, 60, 65, 67, 70-72, 73-79, 80, 82-83, 93, 94

Griffins (gryphons) 46, 56, 58, 63, 65, 73-74, 75, 76

Gruagach (*see also* Fairies) 32, 112

Hermit's Cell, The 8, 82, 89-92

Human sacrifice 38-42

Iona Community, The 10, 48, 54-56, 67, 84, 86

Ireland 9, 15, 18, 19, 20, 21, 34, 40, 43, 44, 59, 93, 99, 111-112

Jacobites 107

Johnson, Dr Samuel 38, 56 65

Lords of the Isles, The 9, 10, 33,

44-45, 46, 47, 53

MacAlpine, Kenneth 9, 44

Macbeth 44, 45

MacKinnon, Abbot John 67, 73-74, 115, 120

Macleod, Fiona (William Sharp) 12-13, 23, 25, 26, 42, 87-88, 92, 97-98, 100, 105-106, 112

MacLeod, Rev. George 10, 40, 42

MacLean's Cross 10, 36, 76

Magdalene, Mary 25

Magic 11, 16, 17, 18, 19, 20, 21, 24, 26, 28, 34, 43, 49, 52, 54, 92, 103-104

Manannan (Celtic God) 92, 100, 115

Martin, Martin 12, 20 42, 43, 46, 50, 52, 53, 54

Mermaids 26, 115, 121

Miracles 17, 18, 19, 36, 49, 88, 93, 94-96, 100

Monsters, Sea 18, 27-28, 38, 100, 106, 113, 119

Mull 8, 22, 31, 36, 41, 53, 58, 74, 83, 106

Munro, Sir Donald, Dean 10, 12, 43

Mysterious events and experiences 17, 18, 72, 91-92, 100, 101-106, 111

Norse mythology 75, 77

Norway 9, 10, 19, 43, 44, 52

Nunnery 29, 33-36, 45, 48, 54, 70-72, 73-79

Ossian 45, 114

Pan 91-92

Pennant, Thomas 12, 24, 42, 43, 65, 78, 80, 98-99

Perthshire 9, 21

Peter of the Gold 31

Picts 15, 21, 23, 36, 44

Pococke, Richard 12, 53, 80, 98

Prophecies 7, 17, 18, 21, 43, 50

Psychic phenomena (precognition, telepathy etc.) 17, 18, 20, 21, 22, 36, 96, 102-105

Reilig Odhráin graveyard 9, 29, 31, 34, 35, 38-46, 47, 48, 53, 59, 70-72, 73-79, 105

Relics 9, 10, 21, 49, 52

Sacheverell, William 12, 20, 22, 24, 25, 33, 39, 65, 78-79

St Adomnan 8, 9, 15, 17, 18, 20-21, 22, 28, 36, 40, 50, 52, 77, 83, 91, 93, 94-97, 99, 109, 111

- *Life of Adomnan* 9, 20

St Blathmac 9, 49

St Bride of the Isles 20, 87-88

St Columba:

- Biography 8, 13, 15-16, 47

- Legends and folklore 8, 15, 16-21, 22, 25, 27, 36, 38-41, 42, 49, 50, 51, 52, 59, 77, 81-82, 83, 91, 93, 94-98, 99, 107-109, 111-112, 115

- *Life* (Adomnan) 8, 15, 17-18, 25, 28, 36, 40, 41, 50, 77, 83, 91, 93, 94-97, 99, 109, 111

- *Life* (Old Irish) 9, 18-19, 23, 38, 41, 99

- *Life* (Manus O'Donnell) 10, 19, 23

St Columba's Bay 8, 107-111

St Columba's Pillow/Stone 8, 49, 77, 82

St Columba's Shrine 8, 47, 49, 51, 52-53

St Columba's Table 8, 80, 82

St Kenneth 36

St Oran 7, 20, 38-42, 76-77

St Oran's Chapel 9, 42, 45-46, 70-72, 73-79

St Patrick 20, 25, 26

Seal-people 26-27, 92

Sheela-na-gig 33-34

Simulacra 11, 110, 112

Sithèan Beg 95, 97

Sithèan Mor 42, 92, 96-99, 103

Snakes (banished) 25

Spirits and spiritual beings 22, 34, 38, 46, 91-92, 97-98

Staffa 10, 74, 113-121

Stone circles and standing stones 7, 23, 24, 35, 42, 8, 99

Stones, ringing 85, 109

Street of the Dead 29, 38, 41, 45

Teampull Rònain ('St Ronan's Church') 34-35, 48

Traigh an t−Suidhe ('Beach of the Seat') 86

Tràigh Bhàn Nam Manach ('White Strand Of The Monks') 84-86

Treshnish Isles 27, 73

Verne, Jules 119

Vikings 9, 29, 43, 47, 49, 52, 70, 73, 84-85, 91, 119

Virgin Mary, The 20, 42, 50, 65, 76, 77, 88

Visions, dreams, altered states etc. 7, 15, 19, 20, 22, 32, 97-98, 112

Walker, Rev Dr John 12, 43

Wells, holy, healing and mystical 18, 56, 73, 86-88, 92

Whisky distilling 88

Witchcraft 20, 22-33